Information Technology
in the Third World

Westview Replica Editions

The concept of Westview Replica Editions is a response to the continuing crisis in academic and informational publishing. Library budgets for books have been severely curtailed. Ever larger portions of general library budgets are being diverted from the purchase of books and used for data banks, computers, micromedia, and other methods of information retrieval. Interlibrary loan structures further reduce the edition sizes required to satisfy the needs of the scholarly community. Economic pressures on the university presses and the few private scholarly publishing companies have severely limited the capacity of the industry to properly serve the academic and research communities. As a result, many manuscripts dealing with important subjects, often representing the highest level of scholarship, are no longer economically viable publishing projects--or, if accepted for publication, are typically subject to lead times ranging from one to three years.

Westview Replica Editions are our practical solution to the problem. We accept a manuscript in camera-ready form, typed according to our specifications, and move it immediately into the production process. As always, the selection criteria include the importance of the subject, the work's contribution to scholarship, and its insight, originality of thought, and excellence of exposition. The responsibility for editing and proofreading lies with the author or sponsoring institution. We prepare chapter headings and display pages, file for copyright, and obtain Library of Congress Cataloging in Publication Data. A detailed manual contains simple instructions for preparing the final typescript, and our editorial staff is always available to answer questions.

The end result is a book printed on acid-free paper and bound in sturdy library-quality soft covers. We manufacture these books ourselves using equipment that does not require a lengthy make-ready process and that allows us to publish first editions of 300 to 600 copies and to reprint even smaller quantities as needed. Thus, we can produce Replica Editions quickly and can keep even very specialized books in print as long as there is a demand for them.

About the Book and Author

Information Technology in the Third World: Can I.T. Lead to Humane National Development?
William James Stover

Mass media, telecommunications, and computer technology can effect change in poor countries, but Third World leaders are often disappointed in the results. Professor Stover looks closely at information technology and communication as agents of economic, social, and political development in Third World countries, stressing that definitions of "communication" and "development" must include participation in the exchange of information and the attainment of humane values. He examines reasons why the current world information order does not meet the needs of the Third World and argues that the major difficulty in achieving the potential of information technology for humane development is a cyclical pattern involving technology and values. When countries acquire the physical means of communication, their leaders are tempted to control them, resulting in censorship that prevents genuine communication. Breaking this cycle is a major requirement in using information technology for development, and Dr. Stover discusses how this may be accomplished practically in developmental, Western, and Soviet contexts.

Dr. William Stover, currently professor of political science at the University of Santa Clara, is the author of *Military Politics in Finland: The Development of Civilian Control Over the Armed Forces (1982)* and *International Conflict Simulation: Playing Statesmen's Games (1983)*. He has lectured on international communication as a visiting professor at the International School on Disarmament and Research on Conflict (a Pugwash affiliate) in Verona, Italy.

Information Technology in the Third World

Can I.T. Lead to Humane National Development?

William James Stover

Westview Press / Boulder, Colorado

A Westview Replica Edition

Published in 1984 in the United States of America by
     Westview Press, Inc.
     5500 Central Avenue
     Boulder, Colorado 80301
     Frederick A. Praeger, President and Publisher

Library of Congress Cataloging in Publication Data
Stover, William J.
   Information technology in the Third World.

   (A Westview replica edition)
   1. Developing countries--Politics and government.
2. Political participation--Developing countries.
3. Communication--Developing countries. I. Title.
JF60.S76 1984   303.4'833'091724   84-16810
ISBN 0-86531-808-5

Printed and bound in the United States of America

10 9 8 7 6 5 4 3

Dedicated to Julius K. Nyerere,
President of Tanzania, a man of wisdom,
compassion, and courage

Contents

x

Tables and Figures

Acknowledgments

The author acknowledges assistance from

The British Museum, London School of Economics,
UNESCO, University of London, and Karl Marx
Memorial Libraries for research facilities

Howard C. Anawalt for ideas and drafts, particularly
on economic development and Soviet communication

Jeffrey M. Capaccio and other political science
students at the University of Santa Clara

Mary Jackson for typing

John and Barbara Christensen for a beautiful, quiet
place in which to write

Diane Elizabeth Dreher for proof reading,
companionship, and love

Introduction

> What improves the circumstances of the greater
> part can never be regarded as an inconvenience
> to the whole. No society can surely be
> flourishing and happy, of which the far
> greater part of the members are poor and
> miserable.
>
> Adam Smith
> in The Wealth of Nations

At 10:00 A.M. the telephone rings in a Zurich bank.
On the line is a financier, thousands of miles away who
wants to buy gold and sell dollars. "We'll take care of
it immediately," says the Swiss banker. Another
telephone call, a computer command via satellite
transfers funds to a New York bank while a second,
similar transaction purchases the gold. The entire
operation takes less than a minute.

The Spanish Civil Guard attempts a coup. Television coverage of the action is broadcast throughout
Europe and North America almost immediately via
satellite. The transmission of this information is so
rapid that people in Iowa know about the coup attempt
before Spanish citizens in Bilbao.

An orbiting satellite senses a vast, barren land
560 miles below. The microwave "pictures" are so clear,
the data so precise that an analyst can determine the
likelihood of mineral deposits and direct on site
exploration. As a result, business executives in New
York and London know more about the resources of an
African country than its government.

A computer in Toronto is given data about the blood
cells of an Indian in the Canadian far north. Through a
program developed by medicine's best diagnosticians, the
Indian's doctor on the scene will know in minutes
whether the cells are normal or whether the Indian has a
form of cancer which might ultimately take his life.

This is IT, information technology, which has
revolutionized the way we work, the way we play, even

1

the way we think.   Commerce, banking, entertainment,
service, the assembly line, education, and health are
fundamentally different today from a decade ago because
of information technology, and people are only gradually
realizing the difference IT has made. A combination of
computers, satellites, telephones, radio, television,
and other electronics, information technology is a means
of communication and information management which
provides more effective and more efficient interaction.
IT has become the source of new jobs, industry, and
recreation in advanced countries, producing qualitative
change in the way we live.   This book is about the
prospects of applying information technology to one of
the most difficult problems of our time--national
development in the Third World.

Today, humankind is divided between the rich and
the poor. Within a nation, this inequality is often
obscured for the affluent who live isolated from the
poor. The same ignorance through isolation exists on
the international level with rich countries in the
northern hemisphere, poor countries in the south.   We
all know that there are wealthy and impoverished
nations, that the gap between the two widens yearly.
The means to alleviate this poverty and suffering
remains a mystery, however, even to economists, social
scientists, and statespersons. How can poor Third World
countries create the wealth required to moderate the
ravages of poverty?   How can they develop national
independence and self-reliance to help their own
people?

In the 1950s and early 1960s, researchers and
decision makers focused on mass media as an important
causal element for national development. They believed
that the information disseminated by mass media could be
decisive in the developmental process. Media were
viewed as a magic multiplier which would transform
individuals in less developed countries, westernize
them, and thereby induce modernization. Accepting the
dominant economic paradigm of development, they argued
that mass media contributed to literacy, urbanization,
industrialization, capital formation, and aggregate
economic growth.

Critics rejected this notion in the 1970's.
Defining. mass media information more carefully as
communication, they viewed it both as cause and effect
in a complex set of relations among political, social,
and economic institutions and processes. Information
communicated by mass media might help some people
perceive opportunities they previously ignored, claimed
the critics; but if no opportunities exist,
communication wouldn't create them.

Today, information technology goes far beyond mass
media communication, offering possibilities for change
and new perspectives on development. IT permits rapid

dissemination of ideas, values, and processes; supplements education, science, health care, and culture; provides the potential for two-way exchanges of information to learn what people really need, and manages resources and data to facilitate the production and distribution of wealth.

Information technology and communication are related. Without IT, the means to communicate, communication beyond the interpersonal level would be impossible. With radio, television, newspapers, satellites, and computers, information can be exchanged worldwide and communication facilitated. IT is the machine, communication is the product; IT is the means, communication, the result; IT is the hardware, communication, the software. Therefore, we need to take a fresh look at the relationship between information technology and national development, realizing that IT may be a useful tool in changing Third World countries and alleviating some of their poverty.

In addition to humanitarian reasons, our own interests demand concern about poverty in the Third World, for the well-being of rich nations is directly linked to the economies of the poor, with the two groups becoming increasingly interdependent. The need for primary products, minerals, and raw materials by advanced states is growing yearly. Any disruption in one country caused by an interruption of supply spreads to other nations and has far-reaching consequences. Private investment in the Third World reinforces interdependence, with western banks acquiring a stake in the economic performance and management of less developed countries similar to a creditor's interest in the viability of his debtors.

Our need to be concerned with poverty in developing countries is also strategic. The United States' last two wars were fought in the Third World. Despite a major sacrifice of lives and resources, neither was successfully concluded. Poverty, injustice, instability, and violence in poor countries create a dangerous situation in which the superpowers frequently become involved. These political clashes could easily lead to military confrontation where escalation is unpredictable and fraught with danger.

Clearly, information technology will not solve all the problems of the Third World. IT represents a potential, however, to deal with some of the troubling issues which aid, trade, and investment have not seemed to resolve. Given our economic and strategic interests, we must try to understand any tool that can help. That is the goal of this book. Chapter 1 examines the relationship between communication and development, describing some of the ways it can produce change. Chapter 2 reviews the current world information order and assesses some of the reasons why this order has been rejected by most Third World states. Chapters 3 and 4 discuss the means to communicate, offering some insights on dependence and self-reliance as well as the alternatives and international issues information technology presents. Chapter 5 examines communication values which encourage countries to use information technology for humane development. A conclusion suggests some steps which must be taken to realize the potential IT has for change.

1

Communication and Development

> Here we stand
> Poised between two civilizations.
> Backward? To days of drums and fest'al dances
> in the shade
> of sun-kist palms?
> Or forward?
> Forward!
> Towards?
> The slums, where man is dumped upon man?
> The factory
> to grind hard hours
> in an inhuman mill
> in one long ceaseless spell?
> > Dei-Anang of Ghana

Imagine you are a young person, about fifteen years old, living in one of the world's poorest countries. You live in a one room house, along with your parents and six or seven brothers and sisters. There is no running water or bathroom, no toilet and no stove for heat or cooking. Your diet consists mostly of starches and grains, totaling less than 2,000 calories per day. If you're lucky enough to work, your job would probably be in agriculture where 12 hour days are not uncommon. You're unable to read or write, and you have almost no chance for education or training. In fact, you'd be fortunate to be alive at age fifteen, for the infant mortality rate in the poorest countries is over eight times that in the developed world.

The gap between the riches of the northern hemisphere and the poverty of the south is one of the most fundamental problems of the twentieth century. The people of North America, Europe, Japan, Australia, and New Zealand comprise around 25 percent of the world's population, yet they control 50 percent of its income. On the average, the inhabitants of the richest countries:

- eat one and one half as much food including nearly twice as much protein as the people in the poorest countries;

- use about five to seven times as much clothing;

- are markedly better housed and better provided with sanitary facilities;

- lose about 19 per 1,000 of their newborn babies compared to 160 per 1,000 in the poorest countries;

- have about 45 times as much energy available to them and about 70 times as much electricity;

- have about ten times as many doctors and 15 times as many hospital beds;

- have 200 times as many cars and 60 times as many buses and trucks.[1]

This enormous gap between rich and poor countries has not narrowed. In fact, it seems to be widening, despite aid and investment from some rich countries.

The world of communication is also divided into two segments. The richer nations have well developed information technology, while the poorer countries lag far behind. The relative communication backwardness of many developing nations parallels their extreme economic, social, and individual poverty. Conscientious leaders in less developed countries want to eliminate this poverty, establishing in its place affluence and cultural pride. Communication can play a vital part in reaching this goal.

There are two general ways in which communication serves people. One of these involves person-to-person communication, such as the telephone or telegraph. This kind of communication makes it possible to contact people, make appointments, and plan things. Point-to-point information technology performs common, everyday miracles in industrialized countries. For example, you may want to get together with a friend who lives 40 or 50 miles away. If you call that person on the telephone, the two of you can agree to meet at a small Japanese restaurant at seven o'clock next Saturday night. Sure enough, on Saturday night he is there, waiting for you. Of all of the hundreds of thousands of potential people and places, he is there at the agreed on time. This is completely dependent upon communication capacity. Imagine the difficulty of arranging business, planning new projects, servicing existing facilities, or even contacting associates if such communication means as the telephone were nonexistent. Yet the absence of this type of information technology is the norm in many less developed countries.

The second way communication serves people is through its mass or community form. Unlike the telephone, mass communication is designed to reach large groups of people, usually through newspapers, radio, or television. These mass media circulate news, entertainment, and ideas. They play an important part in generating public discussion and creating national policies. A country or locality which lacks some basic forms of mass communication, either a newspaper or radio, lacks a capacity to develop community projects and deal with community needs. For example, in an industrialized country, it is possible to inform the entire community about the contamination of a water source, the existence of a farm pest, or the organization of a new football league through the use of radio, television, and newspapers. In countries lacking resources, the information will not get out very rapidly, for it must travel by word of mouth.

Leaders of developing countries recognize the importance of information technology in their plans for national development. They seek adequate point-to-point communication and mass media in order to give their countries a fair chance to participate in the modern world economy and alleviate their poverty. Communication is part of the development process because it is essential to planning, education, and the creation of justice and stability.

COMMUNICATION

An agricultural extension agent was lecturing to a group of cattle farmers about the dangers of the tsetse fly. He had brought along a teaching aid used commonly all over the world--a model of the tsetse fly about half a meter in length. After the lecture, a serious member of the audience commented: "What you say about this disease in cattle may be true, but it cannot concern us, because the flies are not so big in our district."[2] Communication may be an essential component of development, but not all human activity aimed at exchanging information achieves its goal. Variables such as language or culture can impede communication, and successful information exchange on behalf of development is a complex phenomenon requiring more than messages alone.

Three basic points about communications and development should be understood. First, direct comparison between advanced and developing countries indicates the relationship between development and information technology. Lack of IT in the less developed countries correlates statistically with their poverty. A striking disparity exists in the number of newspapers, radios, telephones, and television sets available in less developed countries compared with industrialized nations, as illustrated by the following:

Table 1.1
Levels of development and information technology

Countries (GNP per capita)	Daily Press	Radio Receivers	TV Receivers	Telephones*
	per 1,000 inhabitants			
A. Low Group (less than $400)	19.2	56.0	5.4	1.3
B. Middle Group ($400 to $2,500)	19.0	57.2	22.5	15.1
C. Developed Group (over $2,500)	328.0	741.0	338.0	352.0

*excluding China
Source: Sean MacBride et al, Many Voices, One World (New York: UNESCO, 1980), p. 128.

In short, poor countries have fewer means of communication than rich ones, and the lack of information technology correlates with a low level of development.
    Second, communication can facilitate change in less developed countries. An obvious way that information contributes to change is by answering a crucial question or need. For example, suppose farmers needed more water to increase agricultural production. The information that digging down more than ten meters produces ground water may be all the farmers need to know. However, this information would be of little use if shovels were unavailable. Information technology can help organize a development project, letting primitive villagers know that shovels exist, can be ordered, delivered, and used to accomplish the goal of obtaining ground water to increase agricultural production.[3]
    Finally, it is important to note that communication does not automatically produce change. Indeed, some forms of communication, like propaganda, can be designed to inhibit change and maintain the status quo. Communication reinforcing traditional character traits that have helped the poor survive their hardships often

contributes to form an attitude that resists change. "Acceptance," "endurance," "karma," "kismet," or "God's will" may do little to inspire a belief that people can act to improve their lives.

A survey of the literature on communication reveals that many writers have viewed mass media as a fundamental, causal element of development. Daniel Lerner assumed, for example, that mass media are an independent variable in the development process, a magic multiplier for development. Lerner's focus for change was individual attitudes, values, and aspirations. Exposure to mass media would transform individuals, he argued, making people in less developed countries more like those in the west and thereby inducing modernization.[4] Lucien Pye viewed communication as a prerequisite for modernization. It was "the presence of communication which brought about the downfall of traditional societies."[5] Alex Inkeles and R.H. Smith took a similar position when they concluded their six nation study on change with these words: "The mass media were in the first rank, along with the school and factory, as inculcators of individual modernization."[6]

The most influential work on communication and development in the 1960s was Wilbur Schramm's Mass Media and National Development.[7] Schramm accepted the dominant paradigm of development which focuses on economics and showed how mass media contributed to the development of industrialization and aggregate economic growth. It was the duty of advanced countries, Schramm argued, to provide communication expertise, hardware, and software to less developed countries, thus stimulating their quest for modernization.

These writers agreed that urbanization would lead to greater use of the mass media and raise literacy levels. This, in turn, would support economic growth, increase per capita income, and create interest in democratic citizenship, thereby integrating the new societies and achieving stability. As a result, the less developed countries would become modern in the image of America and her Western European allies.

In the 1950's and 1960's UNESCO contributed to the idea that development required poor countries to follow the western communication model. It created a number of "minimum standards" for communication development in which each country was to provide ten newspaper copies, five radio receivers, and two cinema seats for every 100 inhabitants of its population. This became the "threshold" of development. By acquiring these communication devices, UNESCO reasoned, a traditional society would gain new skills and attitudes to enter the twentieth century.[8]

HUMANE DEVELOPMENT: A NEW APPROACH

This early approach to communication and development has been rejected both by scholars and decision makers in less developed countries. The downfall of the Shah was the most vivid example of this rejection, and it led others to question the older assumption about communication and development. In Iran, an indigenous, traditional information system, based on the Shi'ite Mosques and Mullahs, was used to seize power from the Shah and his powerful army. These religious decision makers rejected western modernization despite a decade of imported communication equipment and high economic growth.[9]

Scholars had already rejected the notion that communication by itself is a cause of development, and they leveled numerous criticisms against the early writers. Communication is far from a simple, independent variable, the critics point out. It is both a dependent and independent variable in a complex set of relationships with social, political, and economic institutions and processes. Successful communication may change a person's perception of his situation, but it cannot, in itself, change the situation. Communication can help a farmer to see opportunities he ignores; but if few opportunities exist, communication will not create them.[10] Development requires a change in social and political structures, not just communication. While information is a complementary factor, communication can have little effect unless structural change initiates the development process.[11]

The early writers were highly ethnocentric, the critics charge, viewing the process of development as similar to the western experience. They rejected traditional culture as inferior, believed it had to be overcome, and sought to make less developed countries over in the west's image. The cause of poverty and low levels of development was assumed to be inside the less developed countries. For Pye, Schramm and others, it was bureaucratic inefficiency and corruption endemic to traditional society. Little attention was devoted to external causes for poverty such as colonial economic exploitation or patterns of international trade.[12]

Finally, critics argue that the content of mass media has little to do with development in some poor countries. In Jordan, for example, a 1974 study indicated that 88 percent of the farmers gave mass media as a source for political information while only nine percent mentioned media as a source for agricultural information.[13] Further empirical studies are needed, but this suggests that people are using mass media for purposes other than obtaining information about development.

Despite these criticisms, communication and

development are closely linked, but in ways different and more complex than earlier imagined. What we need, therefore, are new concepts of development and communication as well as new ideas on how they interact. Efforts are needed to define the relationship between overall development objectives and various social activities, particularly education, cultural expression, science, and communication. Only then can the roles which these activities play in overall development be optimized.

Sweden's Dag Hammarskjöld Foundation has summarized a basic new direction. Humane development must aim at creating the whole man and woman, not just increasing the growth of things which are merely means. Humane development must begin by meeting basic needs, particularly those of the poor who make up the vast majority of the world's population. It should go beyond the satisfaction of economic needs, however, dealing with the human necessity "for expression, creativity, conviviality, and for deciding (mankind's) own destiny."[14]

Humane development also requires socio-economic and political transformation at national and global levels. It must aim at agricultural and urban reform, redistribution of wealth and the means of production, decentralization of power, democratization of decision making, self-management, and the curb of stifling bureaucracy. This kind of development goes far beyond urbanization, economic growth, literacy, and the use of mass media. It is a participatory process of social change, intended to achieve both social and material advancement, including greater equality and freedom for the majority of people.[15]

A successful approach to this new direction for development requires at least three elements. First, success will require greater equality in the distribution of resources, information, socio-economic benefits, and material rewards. The priority should be on rural areas, small villages, and the urban poor where the greatest poverty is found, and closing the gap between rich and poor in these areas is vital.

Second, successful, humane development requires self-reliance and independence, with an emphasis on the potential of local resources. Each nation, even each village, should be permitted a degree of control over development and should proceed in its own way as much as possible. In practice, local groups will seek technical information about development problems and appropriate innovations. Government then communicates in response to these locally initiated requests rather than designing and carrying out by itself top down media campaigns intended to indoctrinate. This will require popular participation in self-development planning and execution usually accompanied by the decentralization of many activities to the village level. It will also involve mass mobilization, directed by the decentralized units as well as the central government.

Finally, successful, humane development requires the integration of traditional with modern systems, not a complete breakdown of the old and its replacement by the new. A synthesis of old and new, whereby people can maintain their links to the past, their cultural identity, and their historic roots, is necessary. An example of this synthesis is monarchical, parliamentary government in Sweden, Norway, and Denmark. Kings and Queens provide people with symbols of national unity and tradition, while real power is exercised by prime ministers and cabinets. Another example is the integration of traditional Chinese medicine with the western, scientific approach. Both are useful, and both can exist side by side.

A humane approach to development requires a new concept of communication as well. In the past, developmental communication was used mainly to disseminate information, to make people aware of development's benefits and sacrifices, and to instill a willingness to follow leaders. This was based on the assumption that newly created wealth or ideas would automatically percolate down and "irrigate" the whole society. The results have achieved some benefits for the more advanced sectors of the Third World, but the gulf between rich and poor has not narrowed.

A new concept of participatory, developmental communication is not limited to information, much less to mass media. Communication supplements education, culture, science, and technology, and it should interrelate with these areas to promote social, political, and economic change. Developmental communication must be two-way, where information is shared rather than simply disseminated from the top downward. It must also be horizontal in nature, where relative equals exchange messages and link themselves together, and it must be decentralized so that villages and rural areas can participate. Participatory, developmental communications may be defined, therefore, as a process that involves "understanding the audience and its needs, ... planning around democratically selected strategies," producing, disseminating, and receiving messages, encouraging interpersonal discussions with peers, and feedback.[16]

Information technology and communication have the potential to help poor countries in three broad areas of development: social, political, and economic. Let's examine each separately, although the reader must understand that in reality this analytical distinction is blurred, for the areas overlap. Successful development requires all three areas to progress simultaneously. The painful lesson from Iran demonstrates how economic growth without corresponding political and social development produces instability, terror, and violence rather than justice, progress and humanitarianism.

Social Development and Communication

Social development is the process by which social, economic, and psychological attachments are changed both in groups and individuals. Communication has a major impact on this process. Understood in its broadest sense, communication goes far beyond the exchange of news and messages. It is both an individual and a group activity, deeply rooted in the social milieu, and it includes the transmission and sharing of ideas, facts, and data. According to UNESCO's International Commission for the Study of Communication Problems, the functions of communication in society include the following:[17]

1. Information: the collection, storage, processing, and dissemination of news, data, pictures, messages, opinions, and comments needed to understand and respond to environmental, national, and international conditions. In short, it permits people to make appropriate decisions.

2. Socialization: the creation of a common fund of knowledge allowing people to become effective members of a society. This promotes social cohesion and active involvement in public life.

3. Motivation: the establishment of society's goals and aspirations, and the encouragement of individuals to pursue agreed upon aims.

4. Discussion: the exchange of facts needed to clarify differing viewpoints and to promote interest in public affairs.

5. Education: the transmission of knowledge needed for intellectual growth, character building, and the learning of skills.

6. Culture: the presentation of cultural and artistic works to preserve the heritage of the past, to inspire goals for the future, and to stimulate imagination, aesthetic values, and creativity.

7. Entertainment: the dissemination of drama, dance, art, literature, music, comedy, and sports for recreation and enjoyment.

8. Integration: the transmission of a wide
variety of messages needed to help people
understand and appreciate each other and to
unite in a common social bond.

The potential role for communication in social
development is on two levels, the individual and the
group. On the individual level, human attitudes require
change, i.e. new orientation and motivation, if social
development is to be both possible and tolerable.
Indeed, rapid social change would be most uncomfortable
to a fully traditional person, inhibited by the bonds of
class and status. Without "psychic mobility,"
traditional people find it difficult to move out of
their place in the social order. Without "empathy,"
traditional people cannot understand another person's
situation. Social development requires the ability to
use reason and pragmatism rather than religion and magic
in making decisions; and it needs the establishment of a
more optimistic outlook concerning the utility of
change. In short, social development changes people's
attitudes about themselves and the world. They no
longer regard the physical world as fixed. They see
that it can be understood and managed in terms of logic
and rules that people can learn.
The major means by which "psychic mobility,"
"empathy," reason, and self-confidence can be acquired
is education, and information technology can play an
important part. The growth of IT in less developed
countries, particularly mass media and audio-visual
aids, would provide new opportunities for education.
Communication produces an "educational environment" in
which it is both a means and a subject. As a means or
medium, it permits greater numbers of people,
particularly in rural areas, to be reached with basic
skills. As a subject or body of information, it allows
people to communicate better with each other and gain
more from their social interaction.
There are a number of explicit, reciprocal
relationships between information technology and
education.[18] First, information and communication are
complements of intellectual development. For many
people in less developed countries, the school is
equated with the mass media, and it is through radio
that people acquire knowledge. Even the content of some
programs which are not educational in nature can teach,
showing the possibility of upward mobility, democracy,
and justice.
Second, the large volume of information available
and the collection of information in specialized categories has given people greater access to knowledge and
its application. Ideas such as "the global village,"
"the computer society," and "the video civilization"

indicate the development of the new environment in which information technology and education are all around us. Access to particular kinds of information enables people to use it for problem solving.

Third, broadcasting facilities in many countries have produced interesting and creative educational programs. Some are formal teaching supplements to school or university curricula. Others are more informal, produced for adults in need of technical or agricultural know-how. Some states have separate broadcast channels for educational programs, while others reserve part of their general broadcasting schedule for education. Almost all countries recognize a public interest in educational mass media.

Fourth, information technology, particularly telecommunications, can upgrade the quality of in-school instruction through audio-visual aids. IT can begin to reach out-of-school children, long neglected in rural areas, by radio and teach basic literacy, arithmetic, and skills in health, nutrition, and agriculture to adults. Information technology includes programmed learning machines, used as a dialog partner for students who need additional assistance, freeing the teacher for other responsibilities.

Finally, educational institutions have begun to focus on effective communication in their curricula as the process of learning is itself recognized as an experience in communication. Educators are on the alert for more effective means of interacting with students, establishing a dialectic between students and teachers which promotes a two-way flow rather than a one-way transfer of knowledge. All of these factors have combined to further the reciprocal relationship between education and information technology, making communication more effective.

An example of the educational role of information technology in development is Acción Cultural Popular of Colombia (ACPO), a series of radio programs designed to teach people reading and other basic skills. The association was founded in 1947 by José Joaquin Salcedo, a priest just out of seminary who felt called to teach reading. Salcedo started with a 100 watt transmitter and a few radios which he gave to peasants. In 1949, he acquired cheap war surplus radios in the United States and expanded his audience to 15,000 people. Today, nearly 140,000 people follow the broadcasts transmitted from an antenna on top of a Bogota office building that houses the studio.

ACPO's aim is help people "who want to better themselves individually and socially and who are consciously committed to the tasks of development."[19] The first course is fundamental literacy, and two out of every five listeners become literate within one year. Five intermediate courses include economics and work (how to improve farming), health, practical math, advanced literacy (writing), and Christian belief and ethics.

This is a very successful program, and information technology is central to its operation. However, ACPO doesn't rely solely on radio broadcasting. It has a widespread network of people who follow up with personal, face-to-face communication. It also has a large library, a book store, and a newspaper. ACPO has therefore supplemented a traditional approach to literacy education with information technology. Most probably, it is the combination of new and old which accounts for much of its success.

In addition to fostering attitude change and embracing education, communication also helps to integrate both individuals and groups. For the individual, exposure to mass media and increased communicative activity seem to progress in parallel. With increased knowledge gained from mass media, people seek to share this information through personal social interaction. In turn, they require further knowledge to continue the interaction. As a result, the process deepens and extends the individual into a circle of interaction which promotes greater integration in the community.[20]

The role of the media in group integration has long been recognized. As early as 1840, de Tocqueville argued that the press made possible the crystallization of public opinion and the consensus essential to democracy.[21] Lazarsfeld and Merton later wrote that the function of the media was "the enforcement of social norms."[22] Janowitz examined the role of small, weekly neighborhood presses in the maintenance of social structure and found that group consensus during rapid urban growth was associated with the development of mass media.[23]

More recently sociologists have suggested that communication affects social integration by providing symbols, categories of meaning, new and extended universes of discourse, and reference group identification, both positive and negative. For example, urban weekly newspapers have helped to develop community involvement. They provide a means to energize local activity, elaborate social contacts, and integrate the individual and the group into a community structure.[24]

A word of caution is in order, however. Mass media are a necessary but not a sufficient cause for integration. They are merely a tool, and they depend on the existence of an emerging social infrastructure, modern transportation, a common national language, and literacy.[25] In England and the United States, for example, mass media developed only after the social structure had laid the foundation of social integration. THe media did not cause integration, therefore, but they did further advance it.

One aspect of social development involves culture, the creativity through which human beings add to nature. Communication is a carrier of culture, basic to the development of community and nation. Mass media are cultural instruments which can work in different directions, however. On the one hand, they can preserve a nation's indigenous culture and its links with the past. On the other hand, media can intrude, eroding a country's indigenous culture and presenting images which are offensive and foreign. This has been called "cultural invasion," and it often reflects alien life styles and values.

Some people in less developed countries welcome certain alien values as liberating. Many educated women in the Middle East, for example, delight in the freedom expressed by European and American women in films and on television. Others in the same culture reject these new values, charging that they lead to disruption rather than liberation. People's exposure to new values and their differing reactions can break down social integration and lead to disorder. For this reason, some less developed countries are critical of imported films and television programs from the west.

Rather than barring western programs completely, the less developed countries need to take a more positive approach. While limiting the more offensive imports, they should revive their indigenous culture, encouraging national film makers, musicians, dancers, and writers. These artists should perform their work in the mass media, emphasizing common cultural elements in the population and the aesthetic traditions of the nation.

Communication and information technology have the potential to aid poor countries in their quest for social change. For the individual, mass media, especially radio and audio-visual technology, assist in education and attitude change. Forms of "small" media such as community newspapers are associated with group integration, and mass media have the potential to support indigenous culture. In short, communication can complement existing institutions and procedures to assist in social development.

Economic Development and Communication

Increased economic activity is a prerequisite for developing countries to care for their people and achieve genuine independence. Without productive agriculture, an economic infrastructure, capital, labor, and industry to meet basic needs, less developed countries can never solve their problems and participate on an equal basis in the community of nations. Information technology and communication play important supportive roles in Third World economies as they do currently in advanced states. Before assessing the nature of this support, however, it is necessary to review differing approaches to economic development and the strategies they present for reducing poverty.

In the 1950s and early 1960s, one economic approach viewed development in terms of rapid growth and industrialization brought about largely through foreign aid and investment. Once a country reached a sufficient level of economic activity, it would enter a "take-off" stage in which further, accelerated growth would propel the country into modernity.[26] This approach served as the model for United States foreign aid programs as it sought to create the preconditions for American style democracy in the Third World.

Toward the end of the 1960s, however, a series of events occurred in states where development seemed to have reached the "take-off" stage. The civil war in Nigeria and the disintegration of Pakistan symbolized "development disasters" and called into question "take-off" economics. The old approach was labeled bankrupt, and some economists recognized the need for a wholly new doctrine.[27] These reformist economists argued that "more than a decade of rapid economic growth in underdeveloped countries has been of little or no benefit to perhaps a third of the population."[28] Even worse, rapid economic growth, industrialization, foreign aid, and investment seemed to be accompanied by "an absolute as well as a relative decline of the average income of the very poor."[29] Indeed, a study of ten Asian countries which account for some 70 percent of the non-socialist, Third World poor showed a decline in real income and wages since 1960. In six of these countries for which data was available, wealth was highly concentrated: 20 percent of the households received 50 percent of the income while the poorest 20 percent got between seven percent (in Bangladesh) and 3.8 percent (in the Philippines).[30]

The reasons for poverty in the Third World are complex, of course, but the reformists focused on inadequate distribution of assets as well as limited access to capital as an explanation for impoverishment. In most poor states, the economic surplus is in very few hands. Its disposal largely determines the pace and the composition of economic growth. The upper income groups' decision to save or consume affects the rate of capital accumulation, and the pattern of demand, strongly influenced by the distribution of income, determines the sectors to which investment flows. Moreover, the urban elite who have access to organized capital markets can obtain finance capital on comparatively favorable terms, and they tend to invest in capital intensive sectors. In short, relatively cheap finance capital leads to the adoption of excessively mechanized technology, higher productivity of labor, higher wages, and a consequent reduction in the quantity of labor demanded. Instead of investing in projects which benefit the rural poor, wealthy citizens in less developed countries often purchase consumer goods or invest in the manufacture of export items to earn foreign exchange for imports.

The solution to poverty, according to these reformist economists, is redistribution of income and investment assets to the poor, land reform, and education. Only through reforms such as these, directed by the government, can the poor increase their income and develop the economy in a way that meets basic needs. Access to investment capital will permit the poor to encourage economic activity that solves their problems. Land reform will give them a stake in increasing agricultural production, and education will prepare them for newly created jobs. Economic growth is still important, but it must be accompanied by more equitable distribution of wealth.

A third group of economists concentrates on the dominance/dependence features of the Third World.[31] Rejecting both the "take-off" and reformist approaches, they argue that both positions make assumptions that simply do not apply to less developed countries. Both assume a harmony of interest in society which is supposed to favor increased national welfare for all. Both assume that the state is a neutral agent, directing economic growth and reform through redistribution of income. In short, the "take-off" and reformist approaches view development as a non-contentious process, not involving irreconcilable conflicts of interest between advanced and less developed countries or between different social classes within a poor nation.[32]

These assumptions are incorrect, the dominance/dependence economists claim. In the Third World, social classes are in severe conflict so a harmony of interests cannot occur. Moreover, the interests of a social class dominating government does not permit the state to be neutral, and it acts on behalf of the class which controls it. Poverty does not result simply from conditions in less developed countries but in the dominance of advanced states and the Third World's dependence on them. The "take-off" approach is little more than an excuse for inequality and the dominion of certain classes or countries over others. The reformists in their acceptance of societies' current structures deal with the symptoms of poverty, not with its cause. What's needed is radical, even revolutionary change. Domestically, the poor must acquire control over the state and the means of production; internationally, the less developed countries must create a new economic order. Reform is simply tinkering with an unjust, unequal system.

Revolutions are messy, of course, and Lenin was correct when he said that one can't make an omelette without breaking eggs. The benefits that the poor obtain from revolution are often questionable, for violence imposes enormous costs in human life as well as economic and social dislocation.[33] Moreover, a new economic order has been sharply resisted by advanced states, and less developed countries will have to continue, at least for the present, within the existing international situation.

A nonviolent, populist method for transferring power to the rural poor would avoid costly dislocation yet provide them with the means to influence their own economic future. This is probably what the International Labor Organization has in mind when it states:

> The main prerequisite for (promoting equality and reducing poverty) would ... be an effective, decentralized, and democratic administrative structure to translate policies into decisions and action, and mass participation in the development process by the poverty groups.[34]

Bringing the poor masses into the decision making process is itself a radical, structural change, and it will, no doubt, be opposed by many in the elite. The chance of success would be greater, however, if it were done nonviolently, avoiding the bloodshed and dislocation which accompanies violence. Of course, such fundamental change assumes that an influential part of the elite genuinely seek humane development and are willing to share power to get it. Few countries accommodate this assumption, but without such sharing, there is no chance to solve the problems of poverty.

Clearly, the various approaches to economic development focus on different causes and solutions to the difficulties of the Third World poor. Nevertheless, there are some elements which transcend the controversy. Even if real democracy and mass participation are achieved either through power sharing or revolution, a growing economy will be necessary to reduce poverty. Moreover, the fruits of this growth must be broadly shared by the rural poor through redistribution if they are to achieve more equality and control over their own lives. Information technology and communication can support this process in a number of ways.

Communication and information technology are planning tools used to set national priorities. For example, it is critical for a country like Nigeria to set goals which take advantage both of its oil and its other resources such as arable land. Peter Enahoro, Nigerian editor of Africa Now has commented on his country's need to establish priorities:

Some 90-95 percent of our foreign exchange
derives from oil, and that is dangerous to the
economy. To make matters worse, successive
governments in Nigeria have placed great
emphasis on rapid infrastructural development
of the country. We now have some of the best
roads in the world, but it is questionable
whether the money we spent building new
expressways should have been used that way.
... Nigeria imports millions of dollars worth
of rice, yet we are a tropical country and
could grow our own food. On the other hand,
if we had not built highways, someone would
say, "they have magnificent mechanized farms
but they cannot transport their produce." ...
So there is a debate over whether we have
chosen the proper priorities.[35]

Planning for a developing country involves not only
efforts to increase economic growth but also a careful
questioning of the priorities to be established.
Communication is essential to this process.

One reason why the rural poor have been excluded
from setting priorities is their inability to
communicate their needs effectively. Living in remote
areas without information technology, they are often
unreachable and therefore silent when national goals are
established. Successful planning requires the existence
of mass media and point-to-point communication to reach
agreement on what are a country's basic needs and how
they can be met in ways that are compatible with the
country's culture.

If a Third World state does not know about the
existence of mineral deposits or potentially productive
land, if it does not have a way to assess the value of
these resources, it will be at a distinct disadvantage
in planning. Such knowledge is now attained through
information technology. For example, by means of
passive microwave sensing, satellites obtain information
about crop yields, water, and mineral resources. Less
developed countries will need to rely on this up-to-date
information if they are to plan effectively and set
priorities. If an advanced country has gathered the
information by satellite, Third World states are bound
to present diplomatic and legal claims to the use of
this information in planning.

Once priorities have been established, the
effective management of the development plan requires
information technology. Mass media and point-to-point
communication can inform the public about the plan and
encourage feedback about its adminstration. Computers
are useful in managing the plan, overall economic
growth, and income redistribution. Computer technology
has become an essential tool in advanced countries,

indispensible to administering personnel, evaluating the
combination of productive factors such as labor, capital
and raw materials, and assessing market demand. Similar
management requirements exist in less developed countries, and computers could assist them in making
priority enterprises more productive, increasing
economic growth. Adminstrative decisions in
agriculture, industry, and finance demand extensive,
current information, and data banks could provide this
to Third World countries as they do to managers in
advanced states. Moreover, income redistribution
through taxation requires extensive record keeping and
information processing. Computers can help assure that
taxes are collected, revenues budgeted, and income
redistributed efficiently.

Finally, information technology can assist in
encouraging the decentralized, democratic administration
and mass participation called for by the International
Labor Organization and the fundamental structural
changes demanded by the dominance/dependence economists.
This represents political change in Third World
countries which could lead to greater equality, the
solution to poverty, and a more just society. Let's
examine the support information technology can provide
to increasing democracy and participation through a
discussion of political development.

Political Development and Communication

A third area where information technology can
assist less developed countries is political
development. This is particularly important, for in
many less developed countries politics is a deadly and
divisive activity. It is often the bullet rather than
the ballot that signals political change in poor
countries, where force rather than compromise is the
main currency. Death squads, secret police, human
rights violations through imprisonment, torture, dis-
appearance, or death are common in many less developed
countries, and little can be done to achieve humane
social and economic development when the political arena
is so brutal.

One of the explicit normative premises of this book
is that people should hold and exercise control over
their own development. This control should be based on
democratic processes which guarantee effective mass
participation. This can be done through a variety of
different democratic formats, but it can never be
accomplished by party structures, electoral systems, or
administrative processes that give mere lip service to
the political influence of individuals and groups. In
short, individuals and groups must be permitted to build
their political power, and this right should be

guaranteed, so long as these groups do not use violence against their own governments. Additionally, the democratic structure should be guided by some long term goals that restrain short term impulses of the people, particularly when a majority seeks to exercise its will against a helpless minority. These goals or norms may be stated in some constitutional fashion, or they may be simply rooted in deep and effective traditions. In general, they include such basic human rights as freedom from discrimination, freedom from arbitrary criminal process, and freedom of communication.

What does "political development" mean? The term includes a number of ideas. It is an ongoing process rather than an end result. All countries continue to develop politically even after they reach a post-industrial economy. Moreover, there is no one model or one path to political development on which all countries are moving. Indeed, there are many models of political development, many differing paths. Some may be progressively conservative. Some are oriented toward socialist ideals. Others are closer to liberal values. Still others attempt a combination. Successful humane development does not necessarily mean that a less developed country will become "westernized" and take on the characteristics of Western Europe or North America. Countries must set out on their own paths to develop in their own way. Finally, not all political change is progressive in nature, leading toward humanitarian, democratic ideals. Political change may produce creative, beneficial results, or change can produce political decay in which darker, more authoritarian forces dominate. This book uses the term "development" to describe the former, a humane and democratic process.

Political development has three major characteristics.[36] First, there is an increased centralization of power in the state, coupled with a corresponding weakening of traditional sources of authority. This does not mean that traditional religious or tribal authority is destroyed. In fact, much of the traditional authority is subsumed under the institution of government, as occurred with the creation of state churches in Scandinavia or tribal councils in Kenya. It's clear, however, that a change in the locus of power is characteristic of political development, and the institution of a central government takes on new power and responsibility.

Second, as states develop, their institutions take on a different character. In traditional societies, the institution of tribal chief had many functions. Often he would create, enforce, and interpret law, serve as religious leader, and lead warriors as a military hero. Modern societies are more complex, however, and require a differentiation of institutions along with greater specialization in their functions. One institution will make the laws, another interpret them, yet another enforce them. As a result, institutions become more complex and more rational in the sense that they are run by rules beyond personal favor or privilege.

Finally, political development requires increased popular participation in politics, mass mobilization, and greater identification of individuals and groups with the nation as a whole. People begin to see themselves as part of a nation which they have some ability to influence. This is the democratic ideal which permits people to have some control over their own lives.

It is in the delicate balance between popular participation and centralized state power that order, legitimacy, and authority rest. "Just as economic development depends," writes Huntington, "on the relation between investment and consumption, political order depends ... on the relation between the development of political institution and the mobilization of new social forces into politics."[37] At one extreme, institutions are very strong while popular participation is very weak. Here, one finds an oppressive, authoritarian regime with little concern for democracy and human rights. At the other extreme, institutions are very weak while popular participation is very strong. Here, one finds political chaos, for there are few channels in which participation can be expressed. As a result, workers strike, students riot, and soldiers <u>coup</u>. To have political order, legitimacy, and authority, popular participation must be channelled into institutions which are adaptable, responsible, just, and democratic.

Political development has two basic requirements which communication can assist. First, people and groups must be encouraged to participate in public affairs. This means that social groups and individuals come to understand their own interests and believe that governmental institutions are legitimate places to accomplish at least part of their goals. A sense of public interest beyond the local village or tribe, a feeling of empathy for other participants in the political process, and an acceptance of compromise--these are the prerequisites for genuine participation.

Mass media have the potential to support and encourage participation. Newspapers and, more importantly, radio broadcasts can expose rural people to life beyond the village. Entertainment programs as well as alternative media groups such as small theater or dance troupes help to develop empathy for other ethnic, religious, and class groups participating in the political process, and news about previous successful compromise can convince people that the political system is a legitimate arena for conflict resolution.

Political development is assisted by communication in a second area. Institutions must be developed which have the capacity to articulate the interests of divergent groups, aggregate those interests into mutually compatible programs, and administer policy. The articulation of interests is a product of social integration at the group level which brings together ethnic, religious, territorial, economic, professional, or status oriented people with similar goals, values, and intentions. The emergence of groups to articulate interests depends in large part on the ability of people to communicate with each other. This requires the establishment of an information technology infrastructure with point-to-point telephone and telegraph links, post offices, roads, and specialized periodicals or newsletters to inform group members.

The aggregation of various articulated interests in a society is possible only where a sense of community exists. This means that individuals and groups have learned to communicate with each other and understand each other beyond the mere exchange of goods and services.[38] Interests are aggregated by political organizations, institutions, or procedures for "maintaining order, resolving disputes, selecting ... leaders, and thus promoting community among two or more social groups."[39] Political parties are probably the most effective organizations to begin the aggregation of various group interests into a national program. Aggregation continues in a two or multiparty system through a legislature or congress. In a single party state, aggregation often occurs in the government's or party's higher level of organization. When there is no effective party at all, it is most difficult to aggregate society's various interests, and deep social cleavage is likely. Like interest articulation, the aggregation of interests requires point-to-point telephone and telegraph communication, roads, and postal services. In addition it requires forms of mass media such as newspapers and radio broadcasts to permit a full understanding of competing interests, explain decisions to people, and elicit their support.

Finally, policy must be implemented or enforced by a government bureaucracy. This requires record keeping, tax collection, budgeting, fiscal management, auditing, evaluation of programs, and feedback from citizens. With the use of computers, these tasks could be simplified and made more efficient. Further, appropriate data bases would aid in the evaluation of government policies and projects.

It is clear that information technology has the potential to aid political development by encouraging mass mobilization and citizen participation, and by providing information about the political process. IT is also useful in strengthening the institutions of government, parties, and interest groups through the use of information. The encouragement of popular participation and local initiative is particularly difficult in remote rural areas where people are isolated, far from major roads or rail links. In these situations, radio communication has been especially useful in mobilizing popular participation for development projects. As a result, people are not only provided help in specific areas like health or agriculture, they are also urged to make decisions which directly affect their lives. Some examples of these efforts illustrate the importance of two-way, horizontal communication in generating popular participation and solving development problems.

In Tanzania, 100,000 radio listening groups were formed in 1974 and 1975, mostly in small villages to focus the attention of 2.5 million people on public health, nutrition, and agriculture. These efforts reached approximately 40 percent of the adult population, bringing them together in a common experience, and forging links between the village and the national government. The radio programs and supplementary print materials, produced nationally, directed people's attention to health problems and provided information on solving them. After hearing the radio program, each of the 100,000 radio forums communicated as a decision making group. They discussed the media messages, applied them to their own local conditions, then decided which health activities they wanted to pursue. It was their own choice, and their participation resulted in building latrines, sweeping streets, digging wells, or other sanitation and preventative health measures. In this way, information technology was supportive, encouraging participation and local initiative.[40]

In the Peoples' Republic of China, the idea of "group planning of births" began in one local area in 1971. All commune or neighborhood committee members in the area met annually to assess their demographic situation and decide their fertility goals for the year ahead, including which people would have children and which would not. The idea was soon widely adopted throughout China. Citizens heard about the group planning of births initially through radio, newspapers, or wall posters. Then conferences were held in which visiting delegates traveled to observe group planning, discuss innovations, and decide whether to adopt it for their own village. In a similar manner, barefoot doctors (non-professional health and family planning aids) began in one area and spread horizontally throughout China. People heard about the barefoot doctors through mass communication and then requested to have the program in their own village. The government supported and encouraged the idea of group birth planning and barefoot doctors. They were diffused and implemented through self-help activities, however, assisted directly by communication.[41]

In these examples, information technology was used to encourage participation as well as to solve basic development problems. Radio, magazines, newspapers and, in China, wall posters bridged the gap between village and city, permitting people in remote, rural areas to share a common national experience. Local initiative and locally organized institutions were created, and people participated in them to solve basic problems and make decisions about their future. This is two-way, horizontal communication in support of political development.

CONCLUSION

Development is one of the great issues of contemporary world affairs. Poor countries suffer from problems in trade, population growth, health, nutrition, agriculture, industrialization, and education. Their needs are compelling, and it is in the interests of rich as well as poor countries that their needs are met. Information technology and communication are important elements in meeting the needs of less developed countries. IT can help encourage participation in public affairs while making institutions and procedures more responsive. IT can assist in education and the formation of positive attitudes toward national independence and self-reliance. Finally, information technology can improve the efficiency, equity, and output of the economy.

It is not surprising, therefore, that leaders in less developed countries look to the international communication order for help in acquiring and using information technology. They expect to participate fully in this order but find few opportunities and little assistance for their countries' development needs. As a result, the Third World is highly critical of international communication. Let's examine the existing conditions of world communication in order to understand more fully the criticism of less developed countries.

NOTES

1. Statistics compiled by the World Health Organization as reprinted in the Economist, October 17, 1981, p. 19 and The Development Puzzle, Nancy Lui Fyson, editor (London: Center for World Development Education, 1979).

2. Story told by Andreas Fuglesang in _Applied Communications in Developing Countries: Ideas and Observations_ (Motola, Sweden: Borgström Tryckeri AB, 1973), p. 13.

3. Gordon C. Whiting, "How Does Communication Interface with Change?" in _Communication and Development_, Evert M. Rodgers, editor (London: Sage, 1976), p. 109.

4. Daniel Lerner, _The Passing of Traditional Society_ (Glencoe, Ill.: The Free Press, 1958), _passim_.

5. Lucien Pye, _Communication and Development_ (Princeton: Princeton University Press, 1963), pp. 3-4.

6. Alex Inkeles and D.H. Smith, _Becoming Modern: Individual Change in Six Developing Countries_ (Cambridge, Mass.: Harvard University Press, 1963), p. 146.

7. Wilbur Schramm, _Mass Media and National Development_ (Stanford, Cal.: Stanford University Press, 1964), _passim_.

8. "Communications: What Do We Know?," Research paper no. 9 of the International Commission for the Study of Communication Problems on file at UNESCO headquarters, Paris and the International Institute of Communication, London.

9. Majid Tehranian, "Iran--Communication, Alienation, Revolution," _Intermedia_, vol. 7, no. 2 (March 1979), pp. 6-12.

10. Larry Shore, "Mass Media for Development" in _Communication in the Rural Third World_, Emile G. McAnany, editor (New York: Prager, 1980), p. 20.

11. J.E. Grunig, "Communication and the Economic Decision-Making of Columbian Peasants," _Economic Development and Cultural Change_, vol. 18 (1971) pp. 580-597.

12. Everett M. Rogers, "The Passing of the Dominant Paradigm," in _Communication and Development_, Everett M. Rogers, editor (London: Sage, 1976), pp. 121-129.

13. S.M. Bargnouri, "The Role of Communication in Jordan's Rural Development," _Journalism Quarterly_, vol. 51 (Autumn 1974), pp. 418-424.

14. _What Now? Another Development_, _Development Dialogue_, number 1 (1975), published by the Dag Hammarskjöld Foundation, Uppsala, Sweden, p. 7.

15. Everett M. Rogers, "The Rise and Fall of the Dominant Paradigm," _Journal of Communication_, vol. 28, no. 1 (Winter 1978), p. 68.

16. Everett M. Rogers, "New Perspectives on Communication and Development" in _Communication and Development_, p. 13.

17. These functions are quoted directly from Sean MacBride, _et al_, _Many Voices, One World_ (New York: UNESCO, 1980) p. 14, with the addition of summary words.

18. MacBride, pp. 25-29.

19. Paul Harrison, _The Third World Tomorrow_ (New York: Penguin Books, 1980), p. 275.

· 20. Irving Lewis Allen, "Social Integration as an Ongoing Principle" in _Mass Media Policies in Changing Cultures_, George Gerbner, editor (New York: John Wiley and Sons, 1977), pp. 245-46.

21. Alexis de Tocqueville, _Democracy in America_, Vol. II (New York: Knopf, 1948), pp. 245-46; originally published in 1840.

22. Paul Lazarsfeld and Robert Merton, "Mass Communication, Popular Taste, and Organized Social Action" in Lyman Bryson, editor, The Communication of Ideas (New York: Harper, 1948), pp. 95-118.

23. Morris Janowitz, The Community Press in an Urban Setting (New York: The Free Press, 1952), passim.

24. Allen, p. 224.

25. Alan P.L. Liu, Communes and National Integration in Communist China (Berkeley: University of California Press, 1971), pp. 4-5.

26. The most influential proponent of this approach is Walt W. Rostow, The Process of Economic Growth (London: Oxford University Press, 1953, 1960); The Stages of Economic Growth: A Non-Communist Manifesto (London: Cambridge University Press, 1960, 1971); The Economics of Take-off into Self-Sustaining Growth (London: Macmillan for the International Economic Association, 1963); and Politics and the Stages of Growth (London: Cambridge University Press, 1971).

27. A.O. Hirschman, "Changing Tolerance for Inequality in Development," Quarterly Journal of Economics, vol. 87, no. 4 (November 1973), p. 544.

28. H. Chanery, M.S. Ahluwalia, C.L.G. Bell, J.H. Duloy and R. Jolly, Redistribution with Growth (London: Oxford University Press, 1974), p. xiii.

29. I. Adelman and C.T. Morris, Economic Growth and Social Equity in Developing Countries (Stanford, Cal.: Stanford University Press, 1973), p. 189.

30. Keith Griffin and Azizur Rahman Khan, "Poverty in the Third World: Ugly Facts and Fancy Models," World Development, vol. 6, no. 3 (March 1978), pp. 295-304.

31. This group is best represented by Paul A. Baran, The Political Economy of Growth (New York: Monthly Review Press, 1957, 1962); Samir Amin, Unequal Development (New York: Monthly Review Press, 1975) and Accumulation on a World Scale (New York: Monthly Review Press, 1974); André Gunder Frank, "The Development of Underdevelopment," Monthly Review, vol. 18, no. 4 (September 1966) pp. 17-31 and Latin America: Underdevelopment or Revolution (New York: Monthly Review Press, 1969).

32. Aidan Foster-Carter, "From Rostow to Gunder Frank: Conflicting Paradigms in the Analysis of Underdevelopment," World Development, vol. 4, no. 3 (March 1976), pp. 167-80.

33. P. Wiles, Distribution of Income--East and West (Amsterdam, The Netherlands: North Holland Publishing Company, 1974), pp. 96-105.

34. Employment, Growth and Basic Needs (Geneva, Switzerland: International Labor Organization, 1976), p. 6.

35. "Building a New Africa," an interview with Peter Enahoro, World Press (August 1982), p. 24.

36. See Samuel P. Huntington, Political Order in Changing Societies (New Haven, Conn.: Yale University Press, 1968), chapter on "Political Development and Political Decay."

37. Huntington, p. vii.

38. Karl W. Deutsch, Nationalism and Social Communication (Cambridge, Mass." MIT Press, 1966), p. 91.

39. Huntington, p. 9.

40. B.L. Hall, <u>Development Campaigns in Rural Tanzania</u> (Cambridge, England: International Council for Adult Education, 1975), <u>passim</u>.

41. P. Chen and A.E. Miller, "Lessons from the Chinese Experience: China's Planned Birth Program and Its Transferability," <u>Studies in Family Planning</u>, vol. 6, no. 10 (1975), pp. 354-66.

2
The World Communication Order

> ... The flow of information between states--not least the material pumped out by television--is to a very great extent a one-way unbalanced traffic, and in no way possesses the depth and range which the principle of freedom of speech requires.
>
> Urho Kekkonen
> Former President of Finland

> The media are American.
>
> Jeremy Turnstall

> Cultural dependency means people in our country have to brush their teeth three times a day, even if they don't have anything to eat.
>
> Elizabeth Cardova

For thousands of years, the most important medium for long distance communication was postal service, based on the Roman Cursus Publicus and operating at the speed of a ship or a horse. At the turn of the twentieth century, people still depended primarily on letters and surface transportation to exchange information. The normal turnaround time for communication between New York and London was one month, and the relative slowness of this communication had a direct impact on world events. On January 8th, 1815, for example, General Andrew Jackson led American troops in the defense of New Orleans against an attack by British forces. Jackson's victory galvanized American public opinion and contributed to a resurgence of American self-confidence. The battle was of no consequence to the War of 1812 itself, however, for that war had ended a full two weeks earlier. Because of the slow pace of transatlantic communication, neither the British nor the American commander knew the war was over when the battle was fought.

31

The speed of communication began to change with technological discovery, and one invention followed another with accelerating speed. Sir Charles Wheatstone and Samuel F.B. Morse invented telegraphy around 1840, and the first public telegraph message was transmitted in 1844. The next major advance was transmission of the human voice by wire, the telephone, which occurred approximately 35 years later. Less than 20 years after that, Marconi and Popoff transmitted wireless messages independently of each other. By the 1920s, wireless broadcasting of the human voice, radio, had become a practical reality.

During the same time period, the technology for transmitting visual images was being invented. In 1894, the first movie film was screened, and around ten years later, the first photographs were transmitted by a telegraphic device. Pictures were first televised in 1923, and regular television service was established in the late 1930s. Immediately after the end of the Second World War, television use rose astronomically. There were, in 1945, virtually no television sets in the United States. By 1950, the number of sets in use was about ten million, and today 99.8 percent of American households have at least one television set.[1]

Little changed for thousands of years, world communication expanded rapidly after World War II, and information technology revolutionized the way human beings and organizations exchange messages. It is difficult to grasp this profound transformation, for there is no historical parallel except perhaps the early stages of the Industrial Revolution. There are people alive today whose parents witnessed the introduction of the telephone in the 1870s, and these same people see television pictures sent back to earth from Mars by satellite. Their children accept radio and television broadcasting as the most common form of mass communication which make worldwide events immediately accessible.

Radio and television have a capacity for bringing millions of people into greater awareness of the immediate events surrounding them. These information technologies require no printing, no surface transportation, and no literacy on the part of the audience. Leaders and opinion makers are able to get directly in touch with an audience in a very personal way. President Franklin D. Roosevelt demonstrated this in his first "fireside chat" which was broadcast on a Sunday evening in March 1932. Roosevelt went on the air in the midst of the stampede to withdraw deposits from banks, and most of the seventeen million American families owning radio sets tuned them in to listen to the President speak about the puzzling subject of banking.

Roosevelt's style of speaking was informal and comforting, perfectly suited to the radio medium. "I want to talk for a few minutes with the people of the United States about banking," he said:

> with the comparatively few who understand the mechanics of banking but more particularly with the overwhelming majority who use banks for the making of deposits and the drawing of checks. I want to tell you what has been done in the last few days and why it was done, and what the next steps are going to be.

Roosevelt's aim was to convince Americans "that it is safer to keep your money in a reopened bank than under the mattress." His talk, combined with the swift action of the executive branch and Congress, did restore confidence in American banks. All the officers and staff members of a Kansas city bank sent a letter to the President which commented on the speech: "Hundreds upon hundreds of our customers have remarked upon the fresh understanding it gave them of the condition of the banks and the future of our country."[2] Roosevelt's "fireside chats" were masterpieces of public communication. Today, commercial and political messages (most of which are no masterpieces) have a definite and continuous impact on our lives day in and day out.

During the past two decades, further technological advances have made instantaneous, worldwide communication a reality, producing a communication order which is, for the first time, truly global. This world communication order is informal, to be sure, based mostly on the practice of states and corporations rather than on formal legislation. However, the order is organized sufficiently to permit description and analysis. It is composed of increasingly sophisticated technologies for transmitting messages by means of mass media and person-to-person information technology, controlled by a concentration of transnational enterprises in the rich countries. Two important elements in the world communication order have real impact on the poor countries' need for development: first, massive disparities in the technical means for point-to-point and mass communication; second, the transnational concentration of ownership and control over the means to communicate. Third World analysis of these elements has led to criticism of the existing order. After describing these two elements, we will examine the developing countries' critique.

DISPARITIES

Instantaneous, global point-to-point communication has been made possible through space technology, satellites, and optic fibers. In 1965, the United

States established Intelsat, and in 1971, the Soviet Union created its own Intersputnik which permit worldwide information exchange. Today, these satellite systems have the capability of carrying voice, video, and all forms of data transmission. For example, the improved satellite, Intelsat V can transmit approximately 12,000 simultaneous two-way telephone circuits plus two television channels as well as computer data.

The optic fiber is another new transmission technology which adds to global communication. In 1877, C.V. Boyes shot molten glass out of a crossbow, creating fibers one hundred to two hundred feet long. Boyes saw little use for his fiber at that time, but the same basic material, a long, thin fiber of glass, is now the basis for improved information technology. The glass fiber permits messages to be transmitted directly by light rather than by the flow of electricity in traditional copper cables. A finger-sized optic fiber cable can carry 40,000 telephone calls at once, while two wrist-sized copper cables can carry only 20,000. Systems now being developed will be able to send 274 billion bits of information per second--a speed of transmission which would allow a twenty-four volume encyclopedia to be transmitted from one point to another in approximately six minutes. Already, the Bell system has installed optic fiber telephone exchanges in parts of American cities.

The satellite and optic fiber enhance two-way communication and data transmission, improving the speed and capacity of delivering information anywhere in the world. When coupled with computers, such high speed flow of information makes it possible for many individuals to shop and work without leaving their house or office. This technology has profoundly changed the way in which human beings deal with each other. Distance is no longer an obstacle. What used to be measured in miles is now measured in time, and that measure has been reduced from months to days, from minutes to microseconds. It is now possible to have an instantaneous communication system which links any two points on the planet.

Perhaps the most familiar kind of point-to-point communication is the telephone. In 1980, the International Commission for the Study of Communication Problems surveyed this aspect of the world communication order and found enormous global disparities.[3] Presently there are approximately 400 million telephones in the world, an increase of 1,000 percent since 1945. The expansion of telephone capacity has not been distributed evenly worldwide, however. Of the 33 countries possessing more than one half million telephones, only one is in Africa (the Republic of South Africa). That continent has only 1.2 percent of the world's telephones, South America only 2.1, percent while North America has 49.5 percent. Indeed, 80 percent of the world's telephones are located in ten countries of Europe and North America. Close to one half of the world's telephones are in the United States, where some cities have more telephones than people. Less developed countries have only seven percent of the world's telephones, although they have a combined population of two billion people, 50 percent of the world's total.

The less developed countries also lag behind in postal services, still the largest system for delivering point-to-point messages. The International Commission for the Study of Communication Problems found that existing postal services in the less developed countries are inadequate due to the remoteness of millions of villages and the poor quality of transportation. Some European countries have one post office per 1000 inhabitants, while most African and Asian countries have only one post office for hundreds of thousands of people.

In short, the international communications order has developed an astounding technical capacity for rapid and extensive point-to-point communication. The capacity is greatly unbalanced, however, with most facilities for information exchange in the industrialized states of the northern hemisphere. Development efforts for the poor nations of the south would benefit greatly from this information technology, but currently they do not share in this communication abundance.

Mass media are a very different form of communication from point-to-point information exchange. The latter, a letter or telephone call, for example, typically involves elements of confidentiality and individual decision making. When one person telephones or writes to another, he or she usually controls the content of the message and anticipates that only a limited audience will read or hear it, then respond. In contrast, mass communication aims at a broad audience, and usually certain editorial mechanisms govern the content of a message before it is received by an audience. Point-to-point communications are essentially decision making processes, while mass communication has come to be essentially an informational and opinion making process. Neither individuals nor organizations can survive in the modern world without access to both types of information technology.

Modern mass media exist in two basic forms. The more traditional form is written: books, magazines and newspapers. These traditional forms retain their importance today, although technology is changing the habits of human being, increasing the importance of a second form of mass media: broadcasting and film. To some extent, while world literacy is increasing, there is a parallel tendency for many people to substitute television and radio for the traditional written forms of mass media.

UNESCO has recently surveyed the increase in availability and use of various kinds of mass media. Tables 2.1 and 2.2 describe increases in available media forms and audiences.

Table 2.1
World media increase

Type of Media	1965	1979	Percentage increase
Press (number of copies, daily newspapers)	348 million[a]	453 million	+30
Radio (number of receivers)	524 million	1140 million	+118
Television (number of receivers)	181 million	471 million	+160
Books (number of new titles per year)	426,000	689,000	+62

[a]around 1966

Table 2.2
World media audiences

	1965	1979	Percentage increase
World Population (in thousands)	3,269,154	4,335,000	+33
Daily Newspapers (circulation per thousand inhabitants)	104	134	+29
Radio Receivers (per thousand inhabitants)	207	336	+62
Television Receivers (per thousand inhabitants)	72	139	+93
Book Titles (per million inhabitants)	168	155	-8

Source: UNESCO Statistical Yearbooks (Paris: UNESCO, 1967, 1981).

For the most part, the availability of mass media has increased substantially everywhere in the world.

The most widely used mass media is radio. It reaches people instantnaeously, and the cost both of receivers and broadcasting transmitters is relatively inexpensive. Because of its economy and capacity to reach large audiences, radio has grown rapidly. In 1950, there were fifty countries with no broadcasting facilities, but as of 1973, this number had been reduced to three. Today, there are an estimated one billion radio receivers on earth, an average of one radio for every four persons. The distribution of these radios is summarized as follows:

Table 2.3
Estimated number of radio receivers in use

Areas	Years	Total number (millions)	Per thousand inhabitants
North America	1965	251	1,173
	1975	424	1,793
	1979	476	1,951
Europe (including USSR)	1965	184	273
	1975	277	380
	1979	335	450
Latin America	1965	34	138
	1975	81	249
	1979	105	252
Asia	1965	42	39
	1975	108	80
	1979	169	108
Africa	1965	10	33
	1975	28	70
	1979	35	77
Advanced countries	1965	460	449
	1975	770	687
	1979	924	801
Less developed countries	1965	64	42
	1975	161	83
	1979	216	97

Source: UNESCO Statistical Yearbook 1981
Note: Data does not include China.

Television, the newest mass media, relies the most on modern advances such as satellite transmission. The reason for this lies in the physical characteristics of television. It is broadcast on much shorter wave lengths than, for example, short wave radio. Television waves are not reflected back to earth by the ionosphere as are short wave radio signals. Therefore, when a television station broadcasts, only those receiving sets which are basically in line of sight with the transmitter are able to pick up the signals. A television broadcast from China to the United States, for example, must be sent from a station in China to a rebroadcast station in the United States, in the past by a cable, now by a satellite relay.

In contrast to radio, television is a very expensive media, both for broadcast facilities and for individual sets. The cost of a television set is well beyond the income of most families in the Third World. Even in the Soviet Union, a color television set is very expensive, costing the equivalent of five months' wages. Moreover, the expense of producing television programs is far higher than the cost of producing programs for radio. As a result, less developed countries have far lower usage of television, and the programming that exists tends to be strongly dominated by foreign productions.

Mass media are an important element in the world communication order, remarkable in their ability to reach simultaneously millions of people all over the world. Television pictures of human beings walking on the moon and live reports of major events like Egyptian President Sadat's trip to Jerusalem have become commonplace with these powerful media. Their potential has only begun to be translated into reality. Like point-to-point communication, the mass media are unequally distributed throughout the world.[4] Countries with advanced industrial economies enjoy most of the benefits of modern communications while the less developed countries lag far behind. In short, the world communications order is marked by two extremes. At the one end of a continuum is the lush development of modern communication and computing capacity, information technology which has changed fundamentally the daily lives and expectations of citizens in industrialized states. At the other end of this continuum are rural villages in developing countries where information technology is no better than American capabilities at the time of the War of 1812. These extremes are simply part of the economic disparity between rich and poor nations. Economic power and communication power go hand in hand.

CONCENTRATION AND TRANSNATIONALIZATION

The second element of the world communication order which affects less developed countries is concentration and transnationalization. Throughout history, long distance means of communications have tended to be controlled by centralized powers. On the international level, the controlling parties have been the more powerful governments. When England held mastery of the seas, for example, she had a practical capacity to control much of the communication which flowed between nations. Today, concentration of communication power has shifted from the original basis of exclusive political control by nation states to economic control by powerful industries as well as nation states. International communication tends to concentrate in the hands of transnational, private corporations or state controlled, socialist enterprises.

The reasons for economic concentration in the field of international communications are not difficult to understand. Substantial capital investment is required to organize and run a communication enterprise. This has two consequences. First, the number of people using the media must rise if the process is to be economical, in terms of the cost of serving one person or sending one message. Second, financing and capital equipment tend to be dominated by large scale enterprises which are able to raise the investment funds. It takes a great deal of money, long range planning, and effort, for example, to produce a satellite system. Only a small number of nations or corporations are equiped to accomplish such a project without excessive sacrifice in other areas. Development and installation of new information technology is likely to remain the domain of large, powerful enterprises.

Concentration of ownership facilities is a problem both on international and national levels, forming oligopolies and monopolies in the gathering, storing, and disseminating of information.[5] Such concentration operates in three directions: 1) the vertical and horizontal integration of companies connected with information and entertainment; 2) the involvement of companies expanding into communication. For example, hotel and restaurant chains, airline companies, automobile manufacturers, and mining companies are now involved in publishing, film production, and theater. 3) The merging or combining of various communication industries into huge multimedia conglomerates.

Nowhere is this concentration better illustrated than in newspaper publishing. Since 1940, the number of newspaper groups--ranging in size from two to 80 daily papers controlled by the same owner--has risen from 60 to 168 in the United States. Newspaper "chains" now own more than 60 percent of America's daily newspapers, and the trend has accelerated, as indicated by the following:

Table 2.4
United States newspaper concentration

Year	No. of Dailies	No. of Chains	No. of Chain-owned Dailies
1923	2,036	31	153
1930	1,982	55	311
1935	1,950	59	329
]940	1,878	60	319
1945	1,749	76	368
1953	1,785	95	485
1960	1,763	109	552
1966	1,754	156	794
1971	1,749	157	879
1976	1,765	168	1,061

Source: C.H. Sterling and T.R. Haight, The Mass Media: Aspen Institute Guide to Communication Industry Trends (New York: Praeger, 1978), Table 221-A.

The trend is similar in other advanced industrial states. For example, in 1963 there were 51 British cities with competing newspaper companies, only 43 by 1968, and 37 by 1973. Fifty years earlier, there had been over 500 British cities with competing newspaper firms. Patterns of circulation also indicate concentration of news sources, with nine out of 111 newspapers in Great Britain accounting for 60 percent of the daily circulation.

In 12 Western European countries, there are now fewer daily newspapers than ten years ago, with drops of approximately 30 percent in Belgium, Denmark, and Switzerland, and 20 percent in France. In the Federal Republic of Germany, the number of independent newspapers (measured by editorial control) dropped from 225 in 1960 to 134 in 1973 while the number of newspaper copies sold increased. For Japan, three Tokyo-based newspapers with their subsidiaries in five other cities account for 50 percent of all newspaper circulation, 27 million copies daily.[6]

Concentration in the newspaper industry results from a number of factors which have been operating simultaneously in many advanced countries. These include economic pressures resulting from technological changes in publishing and distribution patterns, competition for circulation and advertising revenue, competition between rival media, rising production costs and decreasing advertising revenue, planned consolidation of newspapers, management and/or labor problems.

Running parallel to concentration of communication industries is transnationalization, the bringing together of differing national products under one enterprise to manufacture and market goods and services. Film companies are a historical example of the transnationalization process. In early times when films were silent, they 'spoke' an international language of story, image, and action. Charlie Chaplin was as familiar a figure in Russia or Germany as in the English speaking world.[7] Later, Hollywood productions became grand spectacles where stars, often adored for their physical beauty rather than their acting talent, could be of any nationality. These films earned their production costs in the American market but made extra profits from foreign distribution, often for many years.

With television, the structure of the film industry has changed, the process of concentration reversed, and production centers divested of their distribution interests due to American antitrust legislation. The result has been the growth of independent producers, but the process of transnationalization has continued. Today, a film or television production can have an Italian director, a British script writer, American actors, and a location in Spain. Co-production by different national film making centers adds to the process of transnationalization.

The film is then marketed like a commodity, and there is a flow from countries rich in financial resources and production experience to countries which simply supply an audience. The volume of film production has little to do with distribution. India and the Soviet Union produce many more films each year than the United States, but American exports of films and television programs surpass those of both other countries combined. The American films are sophisticated, a transnational product, popular among urban elites all over the world with a disproportionate influence on cultural patterns.

One of the richest sectors of the communication industry is advertising, and this business has become heavily concentrated and transnational. While the major advertising firms are based in the United States, advertising has become a huge, world wide activity with an annual expenditure estimated at over $64 billion. More than half of this is spent in the United States, but Britain, France, the Federal Republic of Germany, Japan, and Canada produce yearly more than one billion dollars each in advertising. In the 1960s and 1970s, the number of United States advertising agencies with overseas operation increased from 59 to 260, and 24 of the largest 25 advertisers in the world are American transnational companies.[8]

Concentration and transnationalization also occur in other communication industries. Electronics, computers, the manufacture of radio, television and recording equipment, as well as entertainment and book publishing have broadened the scope of their enterprises to include production, distribution, marketing, and the raising of venture capital on a worldwide basis. At the same time, control over these industries has been consolidated by financial interests in a few of the most advanced states.

Concentration of ownership within nations is not necessarily undesirable. During the greater part of this century, for example, it has been the conscious choice of public policy in the United States to prefer concentration of ownership, monopoly rather than competition, for electric power companies, creating public utilities in the various states. The appropriate level of concentration of ownership is a matter best left to national policy. Transnationalization is neither inevitable nor necessarily undesirable. The cooperation of economic and social resources in differing countries can produce goods and services more efficiently and less expensively. In many fields, such cooperation can make the world richer and bring its inhabitants closer together.

Ownership concentration and transnationalization of worldwide communication facilities presents a somewhat different problem, however. Such concentration of ownership will not necessarily yield to conscious policy choices by individual nations, especially nations which are not economically strong. Transnationalization of communication facilities under such concentration complicates the picture further with the potential for a homogenization of values and culture. Taken together, concentration and transnationalization of communication may lead to a kind of de facto control over smaller nations by economic and cultural complexes which are entirely foreign.

The present order of world communication combines the phenomena of concentration and transnationalization with the global disparities in person-to-person and mass media communication means. As observers from less developed countries examine this order, they see a system of imbalance with the rich in positions of power and influence over the poor. Instead of an order designed to help the majority of the world's population living in poverty, the order of world communication seems designed to perpetuate the disparity and profit the rich. As a result, many spokespersons from the less developed countries have criticized the existing order as unjust and inequitable.

CHALLENGE TO THE ORDER

The developing nations began an earnest assault on the domination of communication by industrialized nations in the early 1970s. Their attacks on the world communication order can be explained in part by examining their recent history which falls into three distinct phases. The first involved colonial domination by the major European powers, and that experience continues to influence the less developed countries' outlook. The second phase was the struggle and advancement of political independence, which culminated for the most part during the period immediately after World War II. The third phase is the attempt to create truly independent nationhood in the post-colonial world. This phase is almost universally described by the single word, "development."

The former colonies need to develop in many ways. They need an economic basis for survival, a just and stable political order, public health facilities, educational and cultural institutions, among others. Believing that many of their problems are due to the colonial past, these nations often condemn the industrialized states, which include their former colonial rulers as well as socialist countries.

The developing nations' challenge to the world communication order is not expressed with any single voice, however, nor is their criticism of the existing order uniform. This is understandable because these countries have such diverse backgrounds and heritages. Therefore, no one spokesperson for the less developed countries makes all the criticisms, nor will all critics emphasize each issue in the same way. Nevertheless, criticism of the communication order has been persistent and sustained, dealing with three basic problems: the imbalance of world information flows, the domination of Third World culture through film and television program exports from Europe and the United States, and the dominance of advanced countries in the development and transfer of information technology.

World Information Flows

The "free flow of information" is a concept linked to the basic human right of freedom of speech and opinion. "Everyone has the right to freedom of opinion and expression," states the Universal Declaration of Human Rights. It continues, "this right includes freedom to hold opinions without interference and to seek, receive, and impart information and ideas through any media regardless of frontiers." Easy to declare, this principle has been difficult to achieve, but the free flow of information is a corollary to this ideal.

Obstacles to the free flow of information are numerous. Some barriers are evident, obvious, and easy to recognize. They include:

> "physical violence and intimidation; repressive legislation; censorship; blacklisting of journalists; banning of books; monopolies established by political action; bureaucratic obstruction; judicial obstructions such as closed hearings and contempt of court rules; parliamentary privileges; restrictive professional practices; ... economic and social constraints and pressures; de facto monopolies (public, private or transnational); inadequate infrastructures; narrow definitions of what is news, and what should be published, and what issues should be debated; and a shortage of professional training and experience. ... Other obstacles can arise from entrenched cultural attitudes and taboos, and from an unquestioned reverence for authority, whether secular or religious."[9]

These evident or obvious restrictions hinder a free flow of information, but other obstacles are also important in preventing free information exchange.

To be truly free, information flows should be two-way, not simply in one direction. However, the concentration of telecommunications facilities, news agencies, mass media outlets, data resources, and manufacturers of communication equipment in a small group of advanced countries precludes a full, two-way flow of information among equals. As a result, the flow of messages, data, media programs, culture, and other information is directed predominantly from bigger to smaller countries, from those with power and technology to those less advanced, from the developed to the less developed world.

The one-way direction of information flow is a result of historical, cultural, and linguistic patterns. In Europe, the larger, more powerful countries like Britain and France still dominate news and cultural exchange. Important events and valuable scientific, economic, or cultural achievements are often unknown when they occur in smaller countries or areas which do not attract global attention. Links from former colonial periods and existing economic ties also influence the direction of information flows. For example, events in Zimbabwe are reported as news in Britain while the French press devotes more attention to the Central African Republic. The Indian reader is probably better informed about British news than events in France or Germany. This pattern is also present in the Americas where the predominant position of the

United States is reflected in the importance given to
news about North America in the Latin American media.[10]

The area of information flow which has received
most attention in the west is news. Western journalists
have become increasingly concerned over the trend in the
Third World toward restrictions and the exclusion of
foreign correspondents. Moreover, less developed countries seem to be experiencing greater governmental control over their domestic media sources. Both trends are
due in part to the increasing number of authoritarian
governments in developing countries where leaders want
neither a free press domestically nor the reporting of
"bad" news from their countries to the outside world.
However, Third World criticism of news flow is much more
complex--and justified--than the complaints of a few
military dictators. Serious criticisms include the
problems of dependence, objectivity, and distortion.

<u>Dependence</u>. An important, non-evident barrier to
the free flow of information is dependence for news.
The four major western wire services--Associated Press,
United Press International, Reuters, and Agence France-
Presse--dominate news reporting. Anglo-American film
agencies, Visnews, Universal Press International Television News, and CBS have special influence as well.
Their worldwide operations give them a near monopoly in
the international dissemination of news, and the world
receives approximately 80 percent of its reports through
New York, Paris, or London. For example, the Associated
Press transmits from New York to Asia an average of
90,000 words daily, while Asia sends to New York only
19,000 words. Although the transmission from New York
is supposed to contain news from the rest of the world,
it is heavily oriented to news from North America and
Western Europe. UPI Television News sends approximately
150 filmed news stories per month from the west to Asia,
while its output from Asia averages about 20 per month.
Visnews transmits 200 stories from London to Asia each
month in contrast to 20 from the Asian mainland and an
additional ten from Japan. In Latin America, the situation is similar. For every 100 news items received in
Venezuela from the United States, that Latin American
country dispatches seven stories.[11]

Mort Rosenblum, formerly editor of the <u>Interna-
tional Herald Tribune</u> and correspondent for the Associated Press, summarizes the Third World's criticism:

> The Western monopoly on the distribution of
> news whereby even stories written about one
> Third World country for distribution in
> another are reported and transmitted by inter-
> national news agencies based in New York,
> London and Paris--amounts to neo-colonialism
> and cultural domination.[12]

Indeed, in many less developed states, the only way to learn about news from a nearby country is to use the western wire services. However, their reports will be aimed at a western audience with little concern about what people in the Third World want to know. Former British and French colonies are particularly irritated that their primary news sources are Reuters and Agence-France Presse, representing what seems to them as neo-colonial dependency.

It is somewhat ironic that the present dominance of the western wire services in news flow has a historical parallel. Sixty years ago, the cartel formed by Reuters, the French news agency Havas, and the German wire service Wolff controlled all American news sent to the rest of the world and all foreign news sent to the United States. Kent Cooper, the former executive manager of the Associated Press, complained about American dependency:

> Reuters decided what news was to be sent from America. It told the world about Indians on the warpath in the west, lynching in the south, and bizarre crimes in the north. The charge for decades was that nothing creditable to America was even sent. ... Figuratively speaking, in the United States, according to Reuters, it wasn't safe to travel on account of the Indians.[13]

Dependency in news flow is opposed by less developed countries today as it was opposed by the United States sixty years ago.

In theory, the concern over the dominance of the western wire services should apply to TASS, the large Soviet news agency. However, TASS is not a target for criticism, primarily because it "doesn't count" as an international news gatherer, despite its large size. TASS is well recognized as a news agency dominated by a particular viewpoint, and it is not given much credit as a real news source like the other four wire services. As a result, the criticism of dependency is limited to agencies from the United States, Britain, and France.

Objectivity and Distortion. Another non-evident barrier to the free flow of information is the western concept of "objectivity" which results paradoxically in a tendency to distort news from the Third World. Some critics believe that real objectivity in western news reporting is impossible because of the journalists' relationships with a market system that ultimately determines what will be transmitted. Most newspapers and broadcasters have only a limited amount of airtime or space that is not devoted to advertising, the argument goes. To fill their "news hole," editors must select what their audiences want or risk losing readers or viewers who keep them in business. This results in cutting back the amount of foreign news or making the stories so simple that the information covers neither the Third World nor the west adequately. Information must grab the audience's attention and hold it. Thus, news about familiar persons, places, or issues finds its way through news channels more easily than news of the less familiar. Efforts to reach mass markets and give the public what it thinks it wants because of economic imperatives thus tend to lower the quality as well as the quantity of what is transmitted.

Despite claims of objectivity, western mass media often distort news from the Third World. Distortion occurs "when inaccuracies or untruths replace authentic facts; or when a slanted interpretation is woven into news reports, for example through the use of pejorative adjectives and stereotypes."[14] News can be distorted when events of no real importance are given prominance and when the irrelevant is combined with important facts. Sometimes news is distorted by taking random facts and presenting them as a whole, assembling partial truths to form the appearance of complete truth. Distortion also occurs when the way facts are presented causes misinterpretation by implication, encouraging an audience to draw conclusions favorable to a particular interest. It results when the way events are reported produces unfounded or exaggerated fears, causing subsequent action by individuals, groups, or governments. Finally, distortion occurs when silence is maintained about facts presumed to be of no interest to the public.

A simple form of distortion involves stressing bad news and ignoring good news about developing countries. Information about the Third World is often biased because of the large amount of time and space spent on reporting catastrophes, corruption, coups, famines, and natural disasters. As a result, distorted images of totally chaotic nations are what the developed world receives about less developed countries. According to Narinder K. Aggarwala, a former Indian journalist and presently a United Nations development officer:

> The media of the powerful countries want to depict the governments of their erstwhile colonies as inept and corrupt and their people as yearning for the good old days. Leaders who uphold their national interests and resist the blandishments of multinational corporations and agencies are denigrated and their images falsified in every conceivable way.[15]

Some examples of this kind of distortion will help readers better understand the criticism. During the invasion of Zaire, the majority of reports emanating from the four news agencies stressed the deaths of 100 white Europeans, while scarcely mentioning that three times as many blacks were also murdered. Reporting from Iran during the overthrow of the Shah provides another example of distortion. American news media routinely characterized the Iranian revolution as the work of religious zealots in cooperation with opportunistic Marxists rather than the reaction of people outraged by a repressive regime. This distortion misinformed the American public and narrowed the range of debate on this important foreign policy crisis.[16]

Television entertainment can also distort the public's image of developing countries, reinforcing news bias. An Indian critic argues that television projects India to millions of Americans as a country infested with snakes, unhealthy and unhygenic, with holy cows and beggars crowding the street. For example, on the January 16, 1976 "Tonight Show" with Johnny Carson, the movie critic Rex Reed described Calcutta as "the end of the world." Pilots won't even get off the airplane now in Calcutta, he continued. They pack canned food and bottled water and sleep in the airplane all night. They won't get out, because "you have to step over dead bodies in Calcutta, and the wells and the pavement of every street are covered with defecation, and elephants roam wild through the mud and the cattle. ..." There was a beggar child whose "left leg had been broken by its mother, so it could beg. They blind their children. They break their arms."[17] This example involves one man's distorted opinion about a Third World country; yet his view was heard by millions of Americans, many of whom will hear nothing else about India. Such a distorted viewpoint is a powerful message which can easily create false images of an entire country.

Much news distortion is due to sensational reporting, selecting items that can be written to play on the audience's emotion, amusement, excitement, or grief. Journalists often report news in terms of controversy, struggle, and violence on the theory that conflict makes the most interesting news. An example of this can be seen during the coup to overthrow Peron in Argentina. Correspondents suspected that the military would seize power six months prior to the event. Many journalists were unwilling to leave Argentina to cover less dramatic stories for fear of missing the coup.[18] As a result, stories concerning other developing countries were not told. They wouldn't have the same dramatic impact as tanks rumbling through the streets of Buenos Aires in a military coup.

A major explanation for distortion involves news values. What is regarded as news is not the same in every country of the world. Basically, a country's definition of news relies mainly on that country's cultural perceptions. A standard cultural value which exists in most of the developed world is the idea of a free market and the accompanying objective of increasing market sales. News for the developed world is largely considered a commodity to be marketed to the public. As a result, editors and journalists take their cues from public tastes and interests. News must be sensational, circulate quickly after an event, contain new information, and represent a departure from the pattern of normal everyday life.

An alternative news value, widely accepted in less developed countries, holds that news should cover more than recent events. It should cover processes, for example, developmental changes occurring over time.[19] Tanzania's efforts to organize a rural health service by using barefoot doctors (paramedics) presents a useful model to other developing countries and is considered important news. Similarly, the development of inland fisheries in Nepal or the establishment of a forest ranger training institute in Honduras are interesting news in Third World countries. These are not sensational events but long term processes vital to national development.[20]

Contrasting news values explain why critics charge that editors and journalists distort news about developing countries and why their claims of objectivity are often suspect. Editors are looking for items which interest a western audience, and fisheries or forest rangers are less exciting to western taste than coups or catastrophes. Giving the public what it wants is one valid news criteria. However, critics argue that journalists also have a responsibility to provide people with what they ought to know. This includes information about the process of Third World development, one of the most important socio-economic phenomena of the twentieth century.

While much attention in the west has focused on the flow of news, there is also criticism about the flow of technical information regarding manufacturing processes, management techniques, and other technological innovations. Such information is sold by transnational corporations to customers globally. Too little technical information flows to less developed countries; the cost of the information is too high; and there is too much restriction. It is ironic, critics say, that the United States government demands a free flow of news but allows companies to regulate the flow of technical information, charge high prices for it, and restrict information that it considers strategic. If the United States really believes in the free flow of information, critics ask, shouldn't this flow include technical as well as news data?

Imbalance in information flows seriously hinders a truly free flow of information. Viewed in this context, the one-way flow of information is "a reflection of the world's dominant political and economic structures which tend to ... reinforce the dependence of poorer countries on the richer."[21] Current industrial and trading relationships present a similar phenomenon. However, communication is a unique industry, affecting the psychological and social framework within which people live. As a result, critics conclude that the quantitative imbalance becomes a qualitative one--a conditioning influence on the mind which leads to cultural domination.

Cultural Domination

The international flow of books, magazines, television programs, films, and other cultural material probably has a greater impact on developing countries than does news flow. During the 1960s and early 1970s the information technology for cultural communication in the form of cinema, radio, and television stations was exported to less developed countries. The broadcast "hardware," particularly in television, required "software," programs to keep the technology in use. There is rarely enough money or technical expertise to produce domestically in a developing country all the necessary materials. Imported materials are economically attractive because purchasing films and television programs from the United States and Western Europe is much less expensive than the costs of producing them in the Third World. A television director in a poor country is tempted to rely on imported programs, reducing the cost of television broadcasting. Consequently, films and television programs began to flow from the west to the less developed states.

In some developing countries, television imports constitute a majority of the programs broadcast. Moreover, foreign programs are often concentrated in prime time where they have the largest audience. Most of the imports are American or British, and they often give viewers a cultural picture which is confusing. Critics have complained that the shows provide models of life and values in the American suburbs to people who can never achieve that level of material well being. Despite this, "Dallas," "Bonanza," and "I Love Lucy" have achieved remarkable popularity all over the world.

These cultural imports have generated many concerns. Imported programs may represent a threat to the quality and value of indigenous culture, alienating people from their own way of life. The cultural tastes of the west are admired by many people in less developed countries. They are imitated and can become adopted norms of human behavior in countries exposed to them. Some critics have called this "cultural invasion," which involves a parochial view of reality, a static perception of the world, and the domination of one world view by another.[22]   In fact, the flow of cultural commodities is predominantly "one-way," from advanced to less developed countries, as the following indicates:

Table 2.5
Cultural commodity exports
(percentage of world total)

Commodity	Exports from Advanced Countries			Exports from Less Developed Countries		
	1971	1975	1980	1971	1975	1980
Printed matter	94.8	90.8	95.5	5.2	9.2	4.5
Printed books	93.0	90.9	95.1	7.0	9.1	4.9
TV receivers	94.9	95.3	85.6	5.1	4.7	14.4
Radio receivers	87.3	79.8	68.1	12.7	20.2	31.9
Sound recorders, phonographs	98.8	92.8	93.2	1.2	7.2	6.8
Photo, camera supplies	98.7	98.0	98.6	1.3	2.0	1.4
Developed cinema film	79.6	78.4	87.4	20.4	21.6	12.6
Automatic data processing equipment	97.8	97.2	97.9	2.2	2.8	1.5

Source: United Nations Yearbook of International Trade Statistics 1980, vol. II (New York: United Nations, 1981).

American research suggests that television programs are particularly powerful, giving the viewer a set of values which contain certain elements of the culture in which they are produced.[23]   When that same television programming is exported to Third World countries, it often introduces western values which contradict the values of indigenous culture.   For example, western notions about alcohol are quite foreign to some cultures.   Western ideas about the relationships between men and women, parents and children, and authority patterns between the state and its citizens differ fundamentally from those held in many Third World countries. Western attitudes about material well being, efficiency, upward mobility, and success are often beyond the realistic grasp of Third World people.   Having seen these values in the mass media, people in less developed countries may aspire to a western life style.   Unable to achieve it, these people have their rising expectations turn into explosive frustration.

The importation of western mass culture into Third World countries may also tend to overpower authentic, local culture. It is difficult for local film makers to compete with Hollywood or New York. This can inhibit the growth of national culture by adapting it to standardized, international patterns of mass culture. As a result, traditional culture may be supplanted by material of inferior cultural quality. In this area, critics are particularly vocal against television entertainment programming with its emphasis on sex and violence.

Many Third World critics also oppose the alien values introduced by commercial advertising. A consumer mentality is promoted in societies where the emphasis should be on saving and production rather than on consumption. As a result, the creation of demands for consumer goods in developing nations produces tension between citizens who feel advertising's manufactured needs and their government which works to promote saving for the accumulation of development capital. It widens the gulf between the elite and the masses, increasing the level of frustration and relative deprivation. It transmits false needs and represents another avenue for cultural domination.

Critics of commercial advertising abound. One of the sharpest attacks comes not from the radical spokespersons of Third World or socialist states but from a moderate American, former ambassador, now professor emeritus, George F. Kennan. Writing about the United States he observes:

> ... the phenomenon of American advertising ... has been permitted to dominate and exploit the entire process of public communication in our country. It is to me positively inconceivable that the whole great, infinitely responsible function of mass communication, including very important phases of the educational process, should be farmed out--as something to be mined for whatever profit there may be in it--to people whose function and responsibility, in fact, are concerned with the peddling of what is, by definition untruth, and the peddling of it in trivial, inane forms that are positively debauching in their effects on ... human understanding. After the heedless destruction of the natural environment, I regard this--not advertising as such but the consignment to the advertiser of the entire mass communication process, as a concession to be exploited by it for commercial gain--as probably the greatest evil of our national life. We will not, I think have a healthy intellectual climate in our country, a successful system of education, a sound press, or a proper vitality of artistic and

> and recreational life until advertising is
> rigorously separated from every form of
> legitimate cultural and intellectual
> communication. ...[24]

Kennan's view reflects many of the criticisms which
Third World spokespersons articulate. Commercial
advertising in mass media is an intrusion into culture,
unhealthy, unproductive, a destroyer of values. It is
simply one more area where cultural domination threatens
less developed countries.

Technological Dominance

A third set of criticisms about the world
communication order involves the dominance of advanced
states in the development and transfer of information
technology. This is covered fully in the next chapter,
but it will be useful here to present the criticism in
abbreviated form. The United Nations Development
Program estimates that 97 percent of technological
research and development takes place in the advanced
industrialized states whose wealth permits the use of
capital for basic research. This technological development is conditioned by markets in the wealthy countries,
of course, as corporations seek new products and processes for their customers' needs. Few if any western
companies do technological research with the requirements of less developed countries in mind. As a result,
new developments in technology are ill suited for poorer
countries.
Information technology is particularly capital
intensive, highly specialized equipment, and only a few
countries are original manufacturers. The United
States, the Federal Republic of Germany, France, Italy,
the Netherlands, and Japan are the main producers of a
full range of modern information technology. Some
developing countries such as Algeria, Brazil, India, the
Republic of Korea, Mexico, the Philippines, and Singapore have begun to produce or assemble IT, often under
license with foreign parties. However, these Third
World countries are unable to progress to state of the
art technology. For example, of the 60 developing
nations involved in transistor manufacturing, few can
produce the "silicon chips" which will make transistors
as obsolete as the vacuum tube. The larger developing
countries with the potential to become producers have
not been able to standardize their production, and the
smaller countries face serious disadvantages of scale.[25]
Critics argue that too little technical information
flows to them, but since the end of World War II, some
information technology has been transferred from the

west to less developed countries. This was promoted by international organizations like UNESCO, aid programs through the American Agency for International Development, and many Third World governments. During this time, however, the emphasis was on the development of hardware for communication infrastructure and the training of technicians. The need to build production organizations for software in the form of films and television programs was often ignored. As a result, western software followed the hardware with the ensuing cultural domination described above.

Critics of the communications order argue that technological transfer has not resulted in accelerated development. Most of the technology transferred, they claim, has been inappropriate, capital intensive technology where labor intensive technology is required. The transfer has not really helped in creating employment or building an indigenous technological ability. Moreover, current technology transfer tends to polarize society between the elite who benefit from capital intensive resources and the masses who do not benefit at all. In effect, it produces wealth for a small elite without eradicating the poverty of the majority.

To less developed states, imperialism is still a reality which colors their concerns, suspicions, and fears. This is particularly true in the area of communications. Critics of the world communication order from the developing world see themselves dependent on western wire services for news about other countries and about themselves. They claim that the news they get is distorted and imbalanced. They are dependent on the west for much of the software they need to use the hardware of cultural and entertainment communication, and its content is filled with alien values, offensive messages, and enticements to consume rather than save. The technology transferred from the west is so expensive and advanced that less developed countries will remain dependent even as they gain some technological sophistication. The need for change is compelling, say critics of the world communication order, although they do not agree on its direction or ultimate goal.

CONCLUSION: TWO DIFFICULTIES

Communication affluence in the north and poverty in the south is a condition that few observers find acceptable in the long run. The advanced northern countries have become interdependent with the less developed countries of the south. Requirements for trade, raw materials, loans, and investments as well as strategic interests link the two hemispheres in a common future. Given their history of colonialism and dependence, Third World countries are understandably suspicious of initiatives or assistance from developed states. How can they be helped when a vast gulf of fear, poverty, and distrust separate the north and the south?

What the less developed countries need, most of all, is the physical means to be self-reliant, the resources and information to develop their society, economy, and polity in their own way. In terms of communication, they initially require information technology appropriate to their needs. Beyond this, they must have, so much as is practical, the means to develop their own communication infrastructure, produce their own software, and manufacture their own basic communication equipment in the Third World. They will be self-reliant, free to communicate, only when they acquire the physical means to communicate.

This presents two difficulties. First, the less developed countries seek independence and self-reliance. It is clear, however, that no country in the contemporary world can be fully independent from all others. The Third World's desire for complete independence is therefore not possible. Obviously, most less developed countries will never have the resources to launch their own communication satellite, manufacture their own computers, and produce all the equipment necessary for modern information exchange. The object, therefore, cannot be total independence for the less developed countries. Rather, it is self-reliance and a lessening of the one-sided dependence which less developed countries experience in relation to industrialized states. Basic communication technology can be produced in the more advanced Third World countries like India and Brazil, linking the developing world through technology transfer and lessening the feelings of neo-colonial dependence. Distrust would also be diminished through greater reliance on multilateral financing rather than bilateral loans and aid. Total independence is not possible, but interdependence based on reciprocity, equality, and mutual respect is an attainable goal.

The second difficulty involves the freedom to communicate, a necessary requirement for humane development. The expression of ideas, feelings, or values by a person or a nation requires the means to communicate, increasingly sophisticated information technology in this electronic age. Presently, less developed countries suffer a poverty of communication means, and they are not free to express themselves and make their messages heard. When a less developed country acquires the means to communicate, however, its government is tempted to control communication sometimes in the interest of development, sometimes in the self-interest of political leaders. The government permits only messages which it deems appropriate, favorable, and

beneficial to its plans and to its politicians. This is
censorship, of course, the antithesis of commuication
freedom.

The difficulty may be expressed as follows:

Figure 2.6
Freedom-censorship cycle

Adaptation of a model developed by Howard C. Anawalt[26]

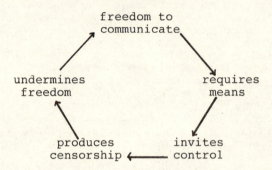

This vicious cycle of represion is the worst kind
because it undermines freedom of expression, a basic
human right and the prerequisite of justice and
liberation. Less developed countries must acquire the
technological means to communicate, then exercise
responsibility in using these means to provide freedom
and democracy for their citizens.

NOTES

1. Television and Human Behavior: Ten Years of Scientific
Progress and Implications for the Eighties, vol. I (Washington,
D.C.: National Institute of Mental Health, U.S. Department of
Health and Human Services, 1982), pp. 1-3.

2. Frank Freidel, Franklin D. Roosevelt Launching the New
Deal (Boston, Mass.: Little, Brown and Company, 1973), pp.
231-32.

3. MacBride, pp. 53-55.

4. MacBride, p. 59.

5. MacBride, pp. 104-05.

6. C.H. Sterling and T.R. Haight, The Mass Media: Aspen
Institute Guide to Communication Industry Trends (New York:
Praeger, 1978); Editor and Publisher, The Fourth Estate, vol. 112
(January 6, 1979), pp. 47-48; UNESCO Statistical Yearbook 1977
(Paris: UNESCO, 1977).

7. MacBride, p. 107.
8. MacBride, p. 109.
9. MacBride, p. 138.
10. MacBride, p. 145.
11. MacBride, p. 146.
12. Mort Rosenblum, "Reporting from the Third World," Foreign Affairs, vol. 55, no. 4 (July 1977), p. 816.
13. Kent Cooper, Barriers Down (New York: J.J. Little and Ives Company, 1942), pp. 12, 43.
14. MacBride, p. 158.
15. Quoted in Elihu Katz, "Can Authentic Cultures Survive New Media?" Journal of Communication, vol. 27, no. 2 (Spring 1977), p. 117.
16. William A. Dorman and Ehsan Omeed, "Reporting Iran from the Shah's Way," Columbia Journalism Review (January/February 1979), pp. 27-33.
17. Quoted in A.W. Singham, The Non-Aligned Movement in World Politics: A Symposium Held at Howard University (New York: Lawrence Hill and Company, 1977), p. 43.
18. John T. McNelly, "International News from Latin America," Journal of Communication, vol. 29, no. 2 (Spring 1979), p. 158.
19. MacBride, pp. 156-57.
20. Narinder K. Aggarwala, "News with Third World Perspectives: A Practical Suggestion" in The Third World and Press Freedom, Phillip C. Horton, editor (New York, Praeger, 1978), p. 199.
21. MacBride, p. 148.
22. Paulo Freire, Pedagogy of the Oppressed (New York: Herder & Herder, 1970), passim.
23. George Gerbner and Larry Gross, "Living with Television: the Violence Profile," Journal of Communication, vol. 26, no. 2 (Spring 1976), pp. 173-76.
24. George F. Kennan, Democracy and the Student Left (Boston, Mass.: Little, Brown, and Company, 1968), p. 231.
25. MacBride, p. 214.
26. The Freedom-Censorship cycle is an adaptation of a model developed by Howard C. Anawalt, Professor of Law at the University of Santa Clara.

3
Communication Means: Technological Dependence and the Goal of Self-Reliance

> Growth must come out of our roots, not through the grafting on to those roots of something which is alien to our society. We shall draw sustenance from universal human ideas and from the practical experience of other peoples; but we start from a full acceptance of our African-ness and a belief that in our own past there is much which is useful for our future.
> President Julius K. Nyerere of Tanzania

> If a man is hungry, you can give him a fish to help him; but if you teach him to fish, he will no longer need your help.
> Proverb

A Swedish development assistance team visited isolated villages in rural Asia to demonstrate population control by means of prophylactics. Using a piece of bamboo, they showed people how to apply the device and seemed satisfied that their message was understood. A year later, when the village reported no decrease in the number of births, the team decided to return for an investigation. Entering the village, they found every house surrounded by bamboo poles, planted firmly in the ground, each covered with a condom. The team had introduced a new technology for birth control, but it remained foreign to the villagers' way of life.

One of the most fundamental problems of development is the integration of technology into traditional societies. Essentially, there are two well established approaches to the organization of national technological resources, the capitalist and the Marxist models. Western economies tend to follow the capitalist approach with its emphasis on the agglomeration of technology and capital in private hands, while Marxist nations place the control of their resources in the trusteeship of the state or party. Most national economies of the world

59

are neither purely Marxist nor purely capitalist in approach, however. They are "mixed," operating with areas of free enterprise and public control over technology and capital.

Less developed countries are trying to move into the twenty-first century with strong economies and self-confidence to serve their people. To do so, they must adopt eclectic strategies of development, using ideas drawn from Marxist, capitalist and mixed models. In most less developed countries, state control over major resources is a necessity in the early stage of development, whatever may take place later on. It is only the state in the Third World which has the power and resources to acquire and integrate technology into society. While doing so, however, the state needs to act responsibly, permitting freedom, encouraging democracy, aiming at humane development.

This represents a basic change from the earlier, post-war concept of development. Instead of reliance on foreign economic aid, there must be more self-reliance. Instead of a purely economic approach, there must be more attention devoted to human elements and greater emphasis on political and social reforms to improve the quality of life. The state needs to foster increased popular participation in decision making and a more equitable distribution of wealth. Technology must be integrated into an indigenous rather than a foreign development model, establishing the genuine self-determination of people.

Some of the major elements of this process have already been suggested. These include basic education, literacy programs, expansion of radio service, and the creation of postal and telecommunication networks to provide communication resources to all elements of the population, young and old, rural and urban, people with widely differing cultural and social backgrounds. The creation of national policies and an international order supportive of these aims will not be enough, however, to change conditions in the Third World. Physical resources, the technological means to achieve objectives, must be acquired by the less developed countries if development is to have even the slightest chance of success.

In short, the freedom to communicate requires information technology, for without IT, there can be no communication freedom. Without the means to communicate, a person's or a nation's message will simply not get through. Communication means increasingly involve modern technology, one of the major moving forces of development. Whether Third World countries seek more efficient communication, more food, improved health care or better education, technology is vital in achieving development goals.

Foreign aid is not necessarily the best way,

however, for developing countries to acquire technological means. While there appears to be no significant objection to the idea that advanced industrial countries should aid the Third World in obtaining modern technology, the prospects for such support are not bright. For the most part, assistance has been meager, created on a bilateral basis, where a single industrial nation establishes a specific assistance program with a single less developed country. Third World countries cannot count on this aid for a sustained period of time, however. American government policy on technical assistance has been distinctly political in nature, for example, subject to change with the dominant philosophy and office holders in the White House and Congress. As a result, assistance has been ad hoc, poorly integrated into over-all development plans. Furthermore, the United States has been unwilling to commit any large sums of money to assistance in communication or information technology, either on a bilateral or a multilateral basis.[1] Other advanced countries have also been hesitant in providing large amounts of assistance for information technology. In any event, bilateral aid often contains political "strings" which attach the less developed countries to the donors, weakening independence and self-reliance. In practice, the transfer of information technology to the Third World is largely in the hands of private, transnational corporations who serve the needs of less developed countries only if it is profitable to do so. However, close integration of the Third World states with the transnational corporations often links their future with western market economies to the disadvantage of many development goals.

Multilateral support arrangements are preferable. However, apart from a few projects, inadequately funded and often poorly administered, there seems to be no substantial ground swell of international support by the industrial world for serious and ambitious multilateral projects to transfer information technology to the Third World. Other methods of acquiring IT must be found. This chapter examines the current state of technological dependence experienced by less developed countries and offers some suggestions for increased self-reliance in acquiring the technological means to communicate.

Technology may be defined as "a system of knowledge, skills, experience and organization that is required to produce, utilize and control goods and services."[2] It is important to development because it is a resource which creates new resources, a powerful instrument of social control, and an influence on decision makers to promote social change.[3] Information technology is unique. Unlike other resources, information is not depleted by its use. It acquires additional usefulness as it passes through a manufacturing system, and it can be used to substitute layers of human management as data on markets and demand are coordinated with data on inventory, production, and supply.[4]

Technology is not neutral. It reflects a certain value system, socio-economic structure, and approach to human interaction which usually get transferred along with the technology. Technology can be both an agent of change and a destroyer of values. It can promote equality of opportunity and income, or it can be used to deny it. Technology influences society, and society's values and organization impose limits on choice and implementation of technology transfer.

The increased use of information technology has consequences which are not always beneficial. One problem is the speed of technological progress, often so rapid that it outruns human capacity to understand its implications and direct it toward the most desirable end. Amadou-Mahtar M'Bow, Director General of UNESCO, expressed his concern about the speed of technological change when he said: "Technological innovation has become one of the incentives to production. What has declined is the mental and cultural ability of society to control the effects of progress. Man no longer endeavors to obstruct the forces of change, but he does not always succeed in taming them."[5] For example, the introduction of television service in poor countries may benefit the urban elite, but the import of foreign films and programs, which seem to accompany television broadcasting in developing countries, can lead to the cultural domination described in Chapter 2.

There are other problems and potentials as well. New information technology carries both the opportunity for innovating creatively and the risk of making the existing communication system more rigid, establishing more powerful, centralized networks. For example, direct broadcast satellites could lead to increased choice and diversification of programming, but they could equally lead to centralized organization, content standardization, and greater cultural invasion through the use of more imported programs. As distance becomes irrelevant because of satellite transmission, the disparities among advanced and less developed countries could diminish. For example, point-to-point communication via satellites could be less expensive than traditional line-and-pole technology, thereby permitting increased person-to-person information exchange in the Third World. Disparities could also increase if these satellite resources are concentrated in the hands of a minority who monopolize their use and maximize their profit. The computer could be a servant or it could be a master, depending on how it's used. Society could be organized on a more bureaucratic, hierarchical basis and social control intensified. On the other hand, the computer could be used to aid the process of development, providing more efficient resource management. In short, technology is not the answer to all problems. It can be a tool to solve some problems, but it can create new ones, as well. Consequently, technological choice must be exercised with great care and foresight.

THE THIRD WORLD'S TECHNOLOGICAL DEPENDENCE

Less developed countries understand the importance of technology to their development, but they are hindered from exercising real choice in formulating their strategies for technological transformation. The international economic system has numerous institutions and mechanisms, many unintended, which keep less developed countries dependent and widen the gap between rich and poor. As a result of industrial concentration, a handful of corporations and government agencies control most sources of new technology. For example, the top 50 American corporations and government research agencies in the fields of defense, space, energy, and health used more than three-fourths of the $38 billion spent on research and development in 1976. The pattern is similar in communication research and development. In the electronics production industry, for example, ten transnational corporations based in five developed countries manufacture most communication equipment, and they account for much of the world's research and development for information technology:

Table 3.1
Corporations and states controlling information
technology, 1979

Rank	Corporation	State	Total Sales (in million dollars)
1	IBM	USA	$21,076
2	General Electric	USA	19,654
3	IT and T	USA	15,261
4	Phillips	The Netherlands	15,254
5	Sieemens AG	Federal Republic of Germany	13,934
6	Matsushita	Japan	10,151
7	AEG-Telefunken	Federal Republic of Germany	7,087
8	Westinghouse	USA	6,663
9	RCA	USA	6,601
10	General Electric, Ltd.	Great Britain	5,953

Source: John M. Stopford, John H. Dunning and Klaus O. Haberich, The World Directory of Multinational Enterprises, vol. II (New York: Facts on File, 1980), pp. 1163-168.

The result of this high level of concentration is a strong oligopoly on new technology. A few hundred people in the advanced countries make decisions on who gets which parts of new technology at the world level and under what conditions.[6] In effect, these people determine which technological resources will be available to support development and how much the technology will cost. Even if one assumes the decision makers' good will and a genuine desire to help poor countries, it is unlikely that they would know what the developing states really need. For example, data bases useful in monitoring development projects must include information about unique conditions in the Third World. How can decision makers in advanced countries understand the conditions completely enough to create information resources necessary for development? Obviously, they can't, and most of their data bases are designed for use by industrialized states.

Nowhere is the disparity between developed and less developed countries more pronounced than in the area of technological research and development. In fact, the dominance of the advanced states is almost total, as indicated by Figure 3.2 and Table 3.3.

Figure 3.2
World research and development

Numbers of R and D scientists and engineers per million population (estimates for 1974 and 1978)   Expenditures for R and D as a percentage of gross national product (1974-1978)

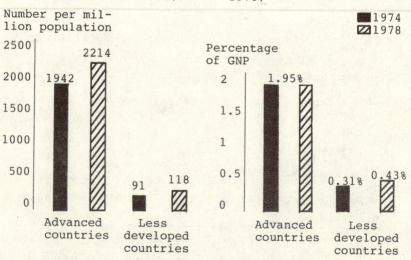

Source: UNESCO Statistical Yearbook 1981

Table 3.3
Indicators of technological capacities
(Percentage of world total)

Indicator	Advanced Market Economy Countries	Centrally Planned Economy Countries	Developing Countries		
			Africa	Asia	Latin America
R and D Scientists and Engineers, 1973	55.4	32.0	1.2	9.4	2.0
R and D Expenditures, 1973	66.5	30.6	0.31	1.63	0.94
Exports of Machinery and Transport Equipment, 1979	85.6	9.6		4.8	

Sources: "Industry 2000, New Perspectives" (New Delhi, India: United Nations Industrial Development Organization ID/237, August 1979), tables 7(1) to 7(4), pp. 180-82;; Statistical Yearbook 1980/1981 (New York: United Nations, 1982), pp. 867-75; Yearbook of International Trade Statistics, 1980, vol. I (New York: United Nations, 1981), pp. 1132-134.

Developing states have only 12.6 percent of the world's scientists and engineers engaged in research and development, 9.4 percent of which are concentrated in a few Asian countries. Third World states use only 2.9 percent of the world's research and developed expenditures and provide only 4.8 percent of the world's machinery and transport equipment exports. There are no comparable data available specifically on research and development for information technology, but there is no reason to suppose that the picture would be much different.

Clearly, this represents technological dependence. It occurs when most of a country's technology comes from abroad. The greater the reliance on foreign technology and the more concentrated the source, the greater the dependence. A country relying on a single source for all its technology is more dependent, therefore, than one obtaining technology from a variety of sources. For some technologies, sources may be widely diversified. For others, particularly information technology, the

sources are highly concentrated. Presently, the United
States is the world's main source of all technology,
supplying between 55 and 60 percent of the flow. For
information technology, however, the figure is even
higher.[7]

Constraints

The international system has certain mechanisms
that perpetuate technological dependence and impose
several constraints on the choices of information
technology open to developing countries. Few advanced
countries consciously seek to maintain the existing
disparities between rich and poor. Nevertheless, the
international business and economic system imposes
certain kinds of competitive behavior necessary for
corporate survival and growth. The results are no less
devastating because they are unintentional. Some of the
most severe constraints are the costs of technology
transfered, the relevance of technology transferred, and
the goals of transnational corporations in the transfer
process.

Technology Costs. International technological
exchange has expanded rapidly, and technology has
emerged as a highly marketable commodity. By 1975 trade
in technology had risen to over $11 billion in lump-sum
payments, royalties and fees compared to $2.7 billion in
1965. Most technology trade occurs among enterprises in
developed countries, with the highest sales in the
United States followed by Switzerland, the United Kingdom, the Federal Republic of Germany, the Netherlands,
France, Belgium, Italy, and Japan. The developing
countries paid an estimated $1 billion for technology
transfers in 1975, less than ten percent of the total
value of all international transactions. Payment to
United States companies from developing countries was
$845 million in 1975, up from $316 million in 1965. Of
this total amount, approximately 50 percent was paid by
Latin American countries, principally Brazil and Mexico,
and approximately 35 percent by Asian countries. The
populous countries of Africa were far behind in
technology transfer.

Competition should reduce the cost of acquiring
technology in a market system. The market in
technology, however, like many others important to less
developed countries is imperfect with monopoly-like
advantages for the sellers who benefit from secrecy and
the protection of trademarks and patents. Technology is
transferred under terms that result from negotiations
between buyers and sellers in situations which are at
least an oligopoly, often approaching a monopoly. The
final price and terms depend largely on the relative

bargaining power of the parties, and the dependent, Third World countries have little power. As a result, the outcome is usually unfavorable for the less developed states. In effect, they must take what is offered them rather than what they really need.

The United Nations Industrial Development Organization estimates that technology imports by developing states could increase from $1 billion in 1975 to over $6 billion by 1985 in terms of fees, royalties, and other payments for technological know-how and specialized services. Much of those payments would go to the industrial countries, representing payment outflow from the Third World and reducing available capital. In some countries, this exported capital will be greater than the imported capital made available through foreign aid.[8]

There is a bright side to the cost picture, however, regarding information technology. Technical change in this area has led to a dramatic decrease in the cost of computers and micro-processors. In fact, over the past 25 years, the cost per computation has fallen 180 times, and a computer which could have cost $1 million a few decades ago now sells for only $300. The cost of performing 1 million calculations fell in one decade from $10 to $.02, and the price of a component now carried on a silicon chip fell from $10 to less than one-fifth of a cent.[9]

This should mean that countries which understand how to use these information technologies could discover a less expensive and more rapid path to development. For example, it is possible to bypass the traditional line-and-pole method of establishing telephone service, to use computers for advanced livestock insemination projects, and to use satellites for remote sensing of mineral and water resources. However, less developed countries need to plan carefully the process by which technology will be introduced. The technology must be developed at a pace consistent with the growth of indigenous expertise, and it must be appropriate to the need it is acquired to fill. Otherwise, technology can create more problems than it solves.

Relevance of Transferred Technology.   Much technology developed in the industrial states has little direct relevance to the needs and problems of developing countries. Most of this advanced technology is not intended to satisfy basic human needs. For example, more than 50 percent of the total global investment in science and technology is spent to produce more sophisticated weapons. About two-thirds of the remainder is directed toward the consumption of non-essential goods. Research and development directly relevant to the basic needs of less developed countries accounts for approximately one percent of the total funds spent on research by the advanced, industrialized states.[10]

Most of the world's ready-made, "packaged" technology is suited optimally to the advanced countries and inappropriate to the developing states. Some western packaged technology has no doubt contributed to social and economic development. However, the transfer of inappropriate technology to the Third World can have many undesirable consequences. In many less developed countries it has increased the gap between rich and poor in terms of earning power and social status by introducing urban employment without corresponding social reform. This has led to a mass exodus from the rural countryside into cities which are increasingly turning into sprawling urban slums. Newspaper, television, and telephone technology tend to benefit the urban elite rather than the rural masses, but they further attract the unemployed to the cities. Predominantly rural countries prefer technology which leads to decentralized rather than centralized production and avoids concentrations of wealth. Most packaged technology does neither. Countries which are labor rich and capital poor want technology that favors maximum job creation with minimum capital cost, but western packaged technology does just the opposite. Advanced technology fosters dependence on foreign capital to purchase it, foreign expertise to run it, and foreign tastes and expectations which result from it. In short, advanced technology can sometimes bring about abrupt and unintended changes in a society, resulting in disruption and destabilization.[11]

Appropriate technology is a response to the problems associated with the sophisticated, western approach. Introduced by E.F. Schumaker as "intermediate technology," it is sometimes called labor intensive or alternate technology as well. Its aim is to concentrate on the simplest technical solution to problems using labor as much as possible. The essence of the approach is small scale technology, using labor skills and local resources to satisfy basic human needs at the village level.

In the field of communication, appropriate technology aims at creating "community media:" small cassette recorders, low power radio stations, super 8 film equipment, half-inch video cameras for television, or mimeographed rural newspapers. This helps avoid the limitation imposed by exaggerated professionalism which is inevitably transferred to less developed countries with the large scale media used in the west. For example, if a developing country tries to start a big television center with links from city to city and signals broadcast throughout the country, it often imports along with the equipment a sense of extravagant professionalism as well, acquired with technical skills through training. Television broadcasting executives in many Third World states demand the same top-of-the-line equipment on which they received training in the west, the same high technical quality of signal programming. This exaggerated professionalism is a limiting factor, inappropriate to conditions in many less developed countries, although it is considered essential in the country where the equipment is produced.

"Big media" technology pushes the society toward centralization and the "trickle down" principle, producing one-way, vertical communication. "Big media" technology makes the less developed countries heavily dependent on western supplies for programs and expertise, furthering a sense of cultural domination. It fosters the creation of a small, alienated urban elite with the accompanying social and economic dislocations. In contrast, small scale media technology tends better to address the developing countries' basic human needs through a less expensive, decentralized, indigenous approach.

There is no real understanding of small scale technology's potential, however, nor of the ways it can be adapted for special use. Decision makers in less developed countries are often unaware of the range of possible choices, and they fail to examine the relative advantages of different types of equipment. Sometimes this is the result of clever sales personnel from the major manufacturers who want to export top-of-the-line equipment. Often the decision makers do not receive promotional material or technical publications about small scale technology. Unfortunately, too many government leaders feel that small scale technology is inferior or second rate. Rural based radio stations rather than urban oriented television broadcasting fail to meet their grand plans to become the technological equals of advanced countries.

It must be remembered that technology is merely a tool. It does not, in itself, solve problems, confer status, or develop a country. In some situations, the best tool happens to be an inexpensive, simple one; in others, it may be more advanced, more costly. The tool must be used for a specific purpose. This takes a well-defined development plan leading to the solution of basic human needs and a careful comparison of available technology with a clear understanding of national goals and interests.

Technology is not neutral in its social, economic, and political effects. Different kinds of technologies can be used to promote various kinds of development and to reinforce power and privilege. All too often, though, advanced, western technology has been used by the elite of a developing country to strengthen their own power position and the coincidental interest of transnational corporations. The introduction of capital intensive technology in less developed countries may increase manufacturing output; for example, earning

foreign exchange that can be used by elites to purchase
imported consumer goods. It can also lead to a loss of
jobs, however, as machines replace people in the
production process. Other kinds of technology might be
more appropriate, leading to greater self-reliance,
increased participation, and the decentralization of
decision making.

Transnational Corporations and Technology Transfer.
Transnational corporations account for approximately 80
to 90 percent of the technology transferred to less
developed countries, and most of the Third World countries depend on transnationals for their own technical development capability. Usually, this has involved "contractual transfers," the major way that less
developed countries acquire technology needed for
science intensive industries like electronic components.[12]

The use of transnational corporations as the main
source of technology has led to many problems. There
has been confusion over basic values and social
priorities, and this has often led to uncritical
purchases of technology without thought about its
consequences. Moreover, the extension of the
technology, management, and productive systems of
transnational corporations into the Third World has
sometimes resulted in the destruction of traditional
technology and the aggregation of social problems. The
kind of development favored by the transnationals
(especially those involved in consumer goods industries
and advertising) does not always respond to social
needs, particularly those of the poor. The
transnationals need growth and expansion with increasing
numbers of buyers. Their capacity to sell is important
to their profits, so they produce and advertise for
those who can afford to buy rather than for those who
need. As a result, they are linked to the affluent
sectors of poor countries, their main local consumers.
They operate on the principle of artificially stimulated
demands through advertising, inducing the purchase of
expensive automobiles, clothes, perfumes, and other
consumer goods. In effect, the transnationals duplicate
the practices of western market economies through
consumption and technology which are often inappropriate
to the real needs of poor countries.

The market power of transnational corporations
determines the availability and kind of transferable
technology in advanced, science based sectors where
technological ownership is held by a few large
enterprises. Because of the high costs of research and
development and the economies of scale involved in
technical innovation and marketing, large companies have
become the major source of technological development and
therefore the owners of the new and improved technology.

In sectors like electronics where rapid technological change reduces the life cycle of capital equipment, the importance of technological advantage makes the control over technology within a corporation vital. As a result, technology transfer is usually conferred only to wholly or majority owned subsidiaries. Where foreign minority ownership is unavoidable, control over technology use is obtained through management or service contracts. In advanced sectors like heavy electronics or telecommunications equipment, the diffusion of technology and competition by rival firms is ·often limited by cross licensing, patent pooling, and other forms of technology sharing among the leading transnational corporations as well as by intra-company technology flows. Therefore, the transnationals provide little relevant technological know-how to less developed countries for their own internal use in meeting basic human needs.[13]

Transnational corporations are not in business to promote development, of course. Their first concern is to earn the highest possible rate of return on investment for their stockholders. If development results from their operation, it is not an unwelcome consequence. However, competitive transnational companies do not risk their capital for altruistic purposes.

There is a real danger here for less developed countries who rely on transnational corporations for the transfer of technology. What the transnationals give, they can also take away. The existing international division of labor rests upon advanced countries supplying technology and developing countries providing labor. When there is no longer a need for labor, however, what will be the comparative advantage of less developed countries? The micro-electronic technology now being introduced in manufacturing firms illustrates this danger.

Micro-electronic technology can offer innovative firms three types of benefits. First, new, improved, and differentiated products can be marketed with substantially reduced lead time. Computerized robots can be programmed quickly to produce and assemble the new items. Moreover, product quality is usually highly improved through the use of robot manufacturing. Second, material utilization is optimized, saving inputs such as energy and steel by combining resources in the most advantageous way. Third, during the manufacturing process, there is savings both in capital and labor. One piece of machinery can be used for many different tasks, reducing or sometimes eliminating labor. Micro-electronics increase the flexibility of production lines, permitting greater variations in product type and often reducing economies of scale.

How will this new technology affect the less developed countries? A recent Institute of Development

Studies Bulletin explores the possible impact of micro-electronic technology on development in a series of articles, with particular attention devoted to international trade.[14] The Bulletin cites the gains which micro-electronics offers user firms in a number of sectors including electronics, design, machine tools, and garment manufacturing. In all but one of these cases, the evidence presented suggests that the introduction of micro-electronics substantially reduces the value to producing firms of situating their operations in less developed countries. Only in the case of machine tools is there some indication that Third World economies may gain some temporary advantage from the introduction of micro-electronics into established product lines; but even in this situation, the advantages are believed to be short lived. Indeed, the conclusion of the various contributors to the Bulletin points to the likelihood of "trade reversal," the relocation of industries which are now in the Third World back to the industrial states.

At the same time that micro-electronic technology is reducing the Third World's comparative advantage, the growing recession in developed states (which also reflects the use of micro-electronic technology in advanced economies) makes it increasingly difficult for the less developed countries to export their manufactured goods. As a result, the future of the southeast Asian electronics industry, until now an engine of substantial growth, is by no means certain. A number of these Asian producers have recently been forced to set up production lines in the United States and Europe.[15]

The same transnational corporations which brought Korea, Singapore, the Philippines, and other Asian countries into the electronics industry through combining high technology and low cost labor now have a new technology which removes these countries' comparative advantage. Dependence on the transnationals in this case has provided short term advantages and rapid growth. The linkage between development and western technology, production and marketing presents, however, the danger of painful withdrawal when the transnational corporations' interests are no longer served.

How can Third World countries react to these radical changes in technology and world markets? Skills are no longer an overwhelming constraint, for the new technology is easier to operate than its pre-micro-electronic counterpart. It is back-up, programming software services that are required, and this means close interaction with suppliers, other users, and buyers. When the software is imported, less developed countries are at a disadvantage, for they are far removed from these backup services. Thought must be given to providing such services, and this has implications for training and education programs as well as the development of a new type of industrial infrastructure. In fact, some less developed countries, particularly India and Brazil, are exceptionally rich in software skills, and a new comparative advantage might be acquired if programming capacities could be encouraged elsewhere in the Third World. Presently, however, the transnationals have introduced micro-electronics in the military sector and in meeting the needs of advanced countries' consumers. Little attention has been devoted to using the technology to satisfy basic development needs, because that would be less profitable than the production of weapons and consumer goods.

Results

The buyers and sellers of technology have different motives and follow different criteria. Suppliers want diverse, free, and lucrative markets in which they can generate revenue from their research and development investments. They try to exploit international financing contracts and join with competitors to retain maximum advantages for profits. The purchasers want to master the transferred technology and exploit it to develop their country. In this conflict of interests, the weaker party, usually the less developed country, often loses. The technology seller can take advantage of a wide range of weaknesses in the buyer's country including lack of capital, appropriate skills, and information.

Technology transfer from the advanced industrialized states has allowed some less developed countries (particularly the more privileged groups within them) to benefit from advances in science and technology. The transfer of technology has enabled these countries to use it without going through the costly, time consuming and difficult process of creating it. Transferred technology has introduced high productivity techniques and in some cases inspired a desire for further development. While there are some real benefits to the present system of transfer, a United Nations report declares, "There are none from the dependency that the process of technology transfer ... and concentration has created."[16]

There are many dimensions to technological dependence. As discussed above, in its most basic expression, it results from the fact that a small number of rich countries are the source of almost all applied technology, and the transnational corporations are almost the sole suppliers. Their motive is profit maximization rather than considerations of development and social welfare. At a more complex level, technological dependence is an aspect of general dependence resulting from a vicious cycle in the operation of the international economic system which governs the association among rich and poor states. Unequal trade relations, unfair commodity pricing, and imbalanced information flows are vestiges of colonialism which reinforce technological dependence. In short, technology transfer may expand industrial output in less developed countries, but it does not necessarily increase the ability of developing countries to adapt and modify existing technology or to create new technology appropriate to basic needs.

Technology dependence is therefore a cause and an effect of general dependence relationships. It leads to greater foreign investment, loss of control over the domestic economy, and the introduction of alien patterns of consumption. This leads toward an "enclave" economy, dependent on advanced countries for markets, management, and finance. The result is the creation of a society in the image of advanced countries, requiring further imports of technology to survive and grow.[17] This vicious cycle maintains less developed countries in a situation of dependence and frustrates their efforts to develop indigenous technological capacities. A different approach based on revised premises and objectives is clearly needed.

TECHNOLOGICAL SELF-RELIANCE

A new approach to obtaining information technology in the Third World must set a goal of self-reliance, reducing the dependency of these countries by building a capacity for producing their own hardware and software. This approach moves away from the "flow" concept of technology toward a "stock" concept. Autonomy in technology does not mean technological independence, however. Just as neutrality or non-alignment requires selective involvement in the international system, technological autonomy will require selective interaction with advanced countries for technology beyond the means of Third World production.

Some Third World spokespersons argue that less developed countries should isolate themselves from western science and technology, that traditional culture "must be protected from the onslaught of western patterns of consumption and those consumer goods that represent the omnipresence of technologies." Developing countries should also "reject all western offers of technological assistance."[18] In a similar pattern, some feel that western news and entertainment programming as well as other forms of western culture such as music and dance should be prohibited.

In some situations, cultural and technological disengagement might stimulate local technological ability and strengthen indigenous culture. This is not really a viable option, however. Clearly the ability to use satellites or large computers requires interaction with foreign technology. Moreover, the freedom for scientists and engineers to exchange information across borders is a prerequisite for technological innovation. Developing countries cannot ignore the international economic system, for it strongly affects individual nation states. If the Soviet Union and the Peoples' Republic of China have found that they cannot isolate themselves from the market economies, less developed countries must realize that complete disengagement is neither desirable nor possible. Self-reliance in information technology does not mean that developing countries need to reinvent the wheel, however. It simply means that they should aim for the capacity to do so, if necessary, and to improve on wheels invented somewhere else.

Technological self-reliance may be defined as "the autonomous capacity to make and implement decisions and thus to exercise choice and control over areas of partial technological dependence or over a nation's relations with other nations."[19] In communication, it is the capacity to identify national needs and to select and apply both imported and domestic hardware and software under conditions that enhance the ability to fulfill these needs. It can be accomplished only when a country understands the dynamics of its dependence and exercises the political will and self-confidence to overcome dependency and nurture cultural identity.

The technology systems of most less developed states are dualistic: a traditional, rural society that contains centuries of know-how exists around a modern urban island, producing for the needs of the advanced countries' markets. Frequently the two sectors operate independently of each other, with the modern sector viewed as progressive and the traditional sector backward. The modern sector usually uses transferred technology, accompanied by values, skills, materials, and organization that are frequently quite foreign to the local situation and the traditional sector. As a result, the traditional technologies become undervalued, underdeveloped, and sometimes eliminated. This has resulted in the atrophy of indigenous technology in the Third World.

There is no simple formula for resurrecting indigenous technology. Overemphasis on small scale technology to meet the needs of the poor may place the country in a second-rate, inferior position. Too much emphasis on sophisticated technology can, as we have seen, lead to greater dependence. Clearly a balance, which uses the correct mix of technologies as a tool for problem solving with the aim of greater self-reliance, is needed between the two extremes.

The goal of self-reliance for technological research and development requires a two-step approach. First, decision makers in less developed countries must choose which foreign technology must be initially imported. This demands a capacity to acquire hardware from a variety of sources and adapt it to local needs. Second, decision makers must fashion an indigenous process of research and development designed to produce new technology for specific needs.

Choice and Adaptation

Developing countries must choose the technology appropriate to their development objectives. Three factors should be considered in making this choice. First, development goals must be clearly defined. What are the objectives toward which the technology will be employed? These may include greater mass participation, social integration, in-school instruction, or adult literacy, for example. Second, an inventory of resource endowments is required. What assets are available to help achieve the objectives? Examples are capital, manpower, skills, and existing technology. Third, the condition of application must be considered. How will the technology be used? This involves both economic and non-economic factors, for example, the degree of infrastructure, the population density and dispersal as well as its social structure, educational background, traditions, values, and culture.[20]

The appropriate technology for a development goal is not necessarily small scale, labor intensive, traditional village technology. Depending on the situation, the most appropriate technology may be very sophisticated indeed, like the SITE satellite education project in India or computer application for large epidemiology studies to improve public health. It is important to remember that technology is merely a tool, conferring no status in itself. Choice simply involves matching the most appropriate tool to the required task.

To choose effectively an appropriate technology, decision makers need both information and the ability to evaluate it. In most developing countries, they lack technical information and don't know where to obtain it. Consequently, important choices of technology are made without adequate knowledge. Where the information is available, the decision makers often lack resources for its evaluation. To overcome this problem, many developing countries have established information centers with the help of UNESCO and UNIDO. Sometimes they are independent organizations, sometimes part of a research institute or other organization. Decision makers in different countries use the centers in varying degrees. In some cases the centers have consulting facilities; in others they are simply small libraries or just a collection of books. To provide decision makers with practical and effective assistance, centers should have information specialists with techno-economic training, and most do not have these resources.

The evaluation of technological alternatives requires both information and skill as well as relevant criteria for judgment. Often these are lacking in Third World countries. Many decision makers think about technology as a constant and often do not consider the criteria to be applied or the impact the technology will have on development.

Adaptation is also a necessary element in acquiring technology. Usually, imported technology is best suited to the factor endowments of advanced, industrialized states; and adaptation is required to match transferred technology to local factor endowments, customs, values, and needs. Industrialized countries can adapt transferred technology into their own technological infrastructure with little difficulty. Less developed countries lack a high degree of infrastructure and find it more difficult to adapt the technology to their own needs. This may require a scaled down version of the hardware and modified software to make it more efficient. Adaptation of technology to master it is an essential part of self-reliance and autonomy.

Research and Development for Indigenous Technology

The capacity to create new technology is not fully understood. It takes more than capital, access to scientific knowledge, and national research centers. The ability to innovate results from interaction among capital and labor as well as information and a scientific infrastructure. It demands cooperation among government and industries, links between the educational and productive sectors, a sound financial base, and the creative energy of a country's population.[21] It also requires the presence of "social carriers," individuals or groups who have an interest in technological application and share their knowledge.[22] Farmers who seek information about new agricultural techniques, for example, may obtain it from radio broadcasts, then communicate their understanding to peers, diffusing or carrying the technology beyond individual application. Furthermore, the ability to create new technology requires government policies aimed at understanding needs and exploiting know-how in the local, traditional communities. Therefore, procedures must be established to facilitate two-way, horizontal communication and cooperation among people in education, business, labor, government, and science. The need to cooperate and communicate must permeate society at all levels: local, regional, and national. The capacity to cooperate and communicate is decisive in creating a climate for indigenous technological innovation. All this demands political will and national self-confidence. It is unlikely that a less developed country could achieve indigenous technological innovation without simultaneous social and political development, for the creation of technology seems to correspond with progressive change.

Every Third World country will not achieve a high level of technological innovation in all areas of communication, of course. There are over 50 less developed countries with very small populations. They lack technicians, engineers, and scientists, and they could never reach economies of scale. Not all Third World countries need to be producers and innovators of technology, however. The poor states face similar problems and needs, and technological innovation in one Third World country may be more easily adaptable in others. Technical cooperation among developing countries (TCDC) is a way to enhance self-reliance for regions and for the Third World as a whole. Specialization through international trade among less developed countries and regional cooperation would permit developing countries to support and encourage each other rather than continue their dependence on advanced, industrialized states. If the transnational corporations will not invest research and development funds for technological applications to solve basic human needs, the less developed countries can do so themselves, creating innovative, indigenous technology and sharing it to solve their own problems.

A call for such cooperation was issued as early as 1955 at the first conference of non-aligned countries in Bandung, when participants spoke about renewing old communication and trade routes destroyed by colonialism. TCDC has been accepted as a goal by the United Nations General Assembly. Regional meetings have been held in Bangkok, Lima, Addis Ababa, and Kuwait to explore possibilities, and a full United Nations conference met in Buenos Aires in 1979 to plan TCDC. Cooperation continues to be illusive despite these meetings and plans. However, efforts to create and share indigenous, appropriate technology could make the goal of TCDC a reality.

Careful choice and adaptation of technology as well as research and development for indigenous technology shared among Third World countries can foster a spirit of cooperation, self-reliance, and autonomy. The less developed countries can thereby reduce their dependence on advanced states and begin to solve the basic problems of poverty. In the words of Julius Nyerere, technology can then be made to serve human need, not human greed.

NOTES

1. Glenn O. Robinson, American delegate to the 1979 World Administrative Radio Conference, states that to the extent the United States government has assisted the development of communication, it has made relatively small contributions through the United Nations Development Program on a voluntary basis. He concludes, "... it has been the source of some embarrassment that the United States in the past has been looser with its promises than with its purse string." "Regulating International Airwaves: The 1979 WARC," Virginia Journal of International Law, vol. 21, no. 1 (Fall 1980), pp. 38-39.

2. "Technological Self-Reliance of the Developing Countries: Toward Operational Strategies," Development and Transfer of Technology Series, no. 15 (Vienna, Austria: United Nations Industrial Development Organization, ID/262, 1981), p. 3, referred to henceforth as Technological Self-Reliance."

3. Dennis Goulet, The Uncertain Promise: Value Conflicts in Technology Transfer (New York: IDOC/North America, 1977), pp. 7-12.

4. Anthony Smith, The Geopolitics of Information (New York: Oxford University Press, 1980), p. 112.

5. An address by Amadou-Mahtar M'Bow, Director General of UNESCO at a closing session of the conference "Information and Society Week 1979" cited in Many Voices, One World, p. 32.

6. Francisco R. Sagasti, "Knowledge is Power," Mazingira, no. 8 (1979), p. 28.

7. Precise figures are not available, but the United States accounted for approximately 70 percent of total world information technology sales in 1975. In some specific areas of communication such as satellites and computers, United States companies possess a near monopoly, although Japan is rapidly developing its computer related exports, particularly large capacity, super computers. See Cees Hamelink, The Corporate Village (Rome: IDOC/Europe, 1977) and "Technological Co-operation Between Developing Countries Including Exchange of Information and Experiences in Technology and Know-how Arrangements" (Vienna, Austria: United Nations Industrial Development Organization, ID/WG 271/1, 1978), p. 3 referred to henceforth as "Technological Cooperation Between Developing Countries."

8. "Technological Self-Reliance," p. 5 and "Towards a Strategy of Industrial Growth and Appropriate Technology" (Vienna, Austria: United Nations Industrial Development Organization, ID/WG 264/1, 1978), p. 4.

9. MacBride, pp. 64-66.

10. Sagasti, p. 28.

11. MacBride, pp. 216-17.

12. "Technological Cooperation between Developing Countries," p. 3.

13. "Technological Self-Reliance," pp. 5-7.

14. "Comparative Advantage in an Automated World," Institute of Development Studies Bulletin, vol. 13, no. 2 (March 1982), particularly Gerald Boon, "Some Thoughts on Changing Comparative Advantage," pp. 14-18.

15. Raphael Kaplinsky, "The Time Bomb in Computers," The Guardian, May 21, 1982.

16. "Technological Self-Reliance," p. 9.

17. Frances Stewart, Technology and Underdevelopment (London: Macmillan, 1977), p. 138.

18. Ziauddin Sardar, Information Consultant at King Abdul Aziz University, Jeddah, Saudi Arabia in "Separate Development for Science," Nature, vol. 273 (May 18, 1978), p. 176.

19. "Technological Self-Reliance," p. 11.

20. These factors are discussed in "Conceptual and Policy Framework for Appropriate Industrial Technology" (Vienna, Austria: United Nations Industrial Development Organization, ID/232/1, 1979).

21. Hans Singer discussed the determinants of a country's technological mix which include both adaption and the creation of indigenous technology in Technologies for Basic Needs (Geneva: International Labor Organization, 1977).

22. Charles Edquist and Ole Edquist, "Social Carriers of Science and Technology," Discussion paper 123 (Lund, Sweden: Lund University Research Policy Program, October 1978).

4
Communication Means: Alternatives and International Issues

> O, what a world of profit and delight
> of power, ... honour and omnipotence
> is promised to the studious artisan!
> ... Go forward ... in that famous art
> wherein all nature's treasure is contain'd.
> Be thou on earth as Jove is in the sky
> Lord and commander of these elements.
> Christopher Marlowe
> in <u>Doctor Faustus</u>

> To say that technology ... creates a new
> environment is a much better way of saying
> that the medium is the message.
> Marshall McLuhan

Technology is a necessary but not a sufficient condition for national development. Other elements must also be present if a country is to employ even appropriate, carefully selected technology to its best advantage. Natural resources, human skills, political will, and a desire for self-reliance are important in fostering sustained development. Without technology, however, development would be at best very slow, at worst, nonexistent.

In advanced countries, information technology has become one of the most important factors in continued development. Between 40 and 50 percent of the jobs in many advanced countries are tied, either directly or indirectly, to information and communication. IT has become a decisive factor in productivity, management, and an expanding gross national product. In some situations, information technology modifies labor; in others, IT replaces it, requiring job retraining and a new approach to the manufacture of goods and services. IT broadens the possibilities of locating productive enterprises in distant areas and permits a geographical diversification of industry. In short, information has become as big a resource as energy or raw materials.

For less developed countries, IT can also play a vital role in development. Mass media are useful in helping to provide education, social integration, political awareness, and the reinforcement of indigenous culture. Satellites and computers can assist in establishing efficient and inexpensive point-to-point communication which permits two-way messages and a better understanding about the needs of the rural poor. IT can also be useful in managing agricultural, health, and industrial development projects.

When considering information technology alternatives, however, a decision maker from the Third World finds a baffling array of possibilities. Let us assume that such a decision maker has clearly defined development goals, realizes the inventory of resources available, and has considered how technology could best be applied. That official still needs to know what various communication means can do for a developing country, the advantages and disadvantages of each, and the problems associated with different types of information technology. Let's consider these questions in an assessment of the technological means available for point-to-point and mass media communication. This assessment must be very general, but it will at least provide a starting point for comparison in the choice of information technology.

MASS MEDIA

The technologies of mass media permit messages to be disseminated to a broad audience, often national in scope. Newspapers, radio and television broadcasting have the potential to reach millions in less developed countries with information vital to development efforts, and the media are clearly associated with public awareness and participation. However, media disparities within less developed countries between urban and rural areas are a severe handicap to effective use.

In Brazil, for example, 440 of that nation's 991 newspapers are published in the states of Rio de Janeiro and Sao Paulo, two of the country's 22 states. These same two states also publish 512 of Brazil's 700 periodicals. 750 of the country's 944 radio stations are in two regions in the south and the southeast, and these two areas have 83.2 percent of the nation's television sets. Of the total radio programming time, only 0.46 percent is devoted to broadcasting for ethnic minorities. Clearly, mass media must be more widely disseminated if they are to serve development needs for the entire country.[1]

In most less developed states, newspapers are not a particularly strong media for reaching the whole nation.

Newspapers that began in colonial societies were originally owned by companies in the mother country and existed primarily to serve the colonialists' information needs and economic interest. Attempts at developing an indigenous press were usually met with repressive measures. Consequently, the years of colonial rule had a tremendous impact on newspapers in the Third World. They were patterned after the European model, financed primarily by advertising, dependent on western wire services for foreign news, and circulated in predominantly urban areas.

Third World newspapers generally have a small and narrowly based audience. UNESCO reports that newspapers and their circulation are not increasing in the Third World. There are eight countries in Africa and three Arab states with no newspaper at all. Thirteen other African countries have only one newspaper each. Compared to one newspaper for every three inhabitants in North America, newspaper circulation averages one copy per 90 inhabitants in Africa and one per 15 inhabitants in Asia. In fact, developing countries have 75 percent of the world's population but only 50 percent of the newspapers and 25 percent of their total circulation. Where newspapers do circulate in the Third World, they are often an elite, urban oriented form of communication. For example, India has 835 different newspapers, but they circulate almost entirely in towns and urban areas. In many other less developed countries, newspapers are published only once or twice each week and hardly circulate in rural areas at all.

Where less developed countries have tried to encourage more widespread use of the indigenous press, they have often experienced competition from the west in the form of rival papers. For example, in Asia there are over 140 English language newspapers circulating mostly in the cities among people who might otherwise constitute an audience for an indigenous press. Some English language papers are locally owned, but many are not, and they tend to take over advertising revenue and readers.

The English language papers are cheaper to produce because they can use more modern printing technology. It takes much more newsprint to publish the same information in most Asian languages than in English. In India, for example, it requires only half the newsprint to produce the same material in English as in the Indian languages. Moreover, when an audience which attracts advertisers is established in Asia, it is often directed to the English language press.

Excluding Japan, Far Eastern newspapers lack adequate financing. The average newspaper in India is supported by $9 worth of advertising, most sold to the government, while the average Japanese newspaper gets $23. The average Asian reader outside Japan must work three weeks to earn enough for a one year's subscription while the average American reader earns the money in 2 1/2 days.[2]

The reasons for newspaper scarcity in the Third World are not difficult to understand. Newsprint is produced in small quantities in less developed countries, and the cost of importing newsprint has increased dramatically in the last decade.[3] The cost of delivering newspapers has also risen sharply as a result of the oil crisis of the 1970s, and the press suffers a further disadvantage because it depends on direct user financing. Sophisticated technology such as computerized typesetting which newspapers in advanced countries use to cut costs is very expensive, beyond the means of most Third World publishers. These high costs, coupled with the large number of illiterates in many less developed countries, reduce the effectiveness of the newspaper as a development media.

Television is also of limited use as a development media. In 1975, UNESCO reported that 30 countries in Africa and Asia had no television service. In some countries which do have television, different languages make it difficult to produce programs which the entire population can understand. The ownership of a television set in many Third World countries is still a privilege possessed only by an urban elite, and the media is therefore narrowly based, excluding both poor and rural people.

Television broadcasting technology has presented less developed countries with special problems. As Third World states introduced television, they sent technicians to advanced countries for training. Returning with an exaggerated sense of "professionalism," they recommend advanced broadcasting equipment rather than more appropriate, less expensive technology such as half-inch video cameras and small gauge recorders. Having purchased large, studio sized hardware, the less developed countries may no longer have the option of adding smaller, less costly equipment to their broadcasting system. Furthermore, lack of standardization has prevented countries from exchanging programs, even within the same region. Color television has added to the complexity. The existence of three basic frequencies and line standards--NTSC, PAL and SECAM--means that countries with different systems find it difficult to share programs. Today, conversion from one standard to another is no longer a technical problem, but it is costly. Where facilities for conversion do not exist, the exchange of programs is impossible.[4]

When this new media first appeared, less developed countries imported both television technology, the hardware, as well as programming, the software from the west. It was simply cheaper to import programs than to produce them. Moreover, the cost of television broad-

casting required many Third World countries to permit
advertising for revenue. The combination of advertisements and western programs led to many of the problems
described in Chapter 2--cultural domination, alienation,
and consumerism. Far from aiding the development
process in most countries, television seems to have created more problems than it has solved.

Radio is the dominant mass media in the Third
World, and its growth demonstrates the potential of
radio as a development communication media. In 1950, 50
countries had no broadcasting stations, 23 of these on
the African continent. By 1960, the number of states
without radio broadcasting facilities had declined to
12, seven of which were in Africa. In 1973, a survey of
187 countries and territories revealed that every
African country had radio transmitters, and only Bhutan,
Lichtenstein, and San Marino were without. Today it is
likely that all Latin Americans and a large majority of
Asians and Africans have regular access to radio
broadcasts.

Radio presents fewer technological problems to less
developed countries. This is due in part to the
standardization of recording type formats, dry cell
batteries, and the agreed upon use of radio spectrum
frequencies. The technology involved in radio broadcasting is rather simple compared to television, permitting almost all Third World states to produce their own
programs. Unlike newspapers, radio does not require
literacy, and messages can be broadcast easily and economically to rural areas in the many languages (some
unwritten) that exist in less developed countries.[5]

Despite these advantages, there are some problems
with Third World radio broadcasting. In some countries,
radio still retains an urban orientation which fails to
meet rural people's needs. Careful attention must be
given to broadcasting in the languages of minorities,
producing the kinds of programs that support development
and insuring that radio receivers are distributed in
remote areas.

Although there are non-commercial stations in
developing countries, many have become commercial in
format, particularly in Latin America. This results in
part from the competition of foreign stations and the
need for revenue to finance broadcasting. Once there is
a demand for the kind of programs that accompany
foreign, commercial broadcasting, that demand must be
filled by the Third World country or its station will
lose audiences. Many developing states lack the
resources to satisfy this demand, however, so they must
import not only the technology but also the commercial
advertising format to finance broadcasting and some of
the programming in the form of western popular music.

Another problem involves the frequency bands on
which radio signals travel. They are assigned by the

International Telecommunications Union (ITU) with Africa and Europe part of the same region for spectrum planning and allocation. In the past, this presented few problems. European transmitters were weak, and few African countries had radio stations. Presently, European transmitters have become more powerful, however, and the use of all radio broadcasting has increased dramatically. As a result, the strong European signals have caused interference with African broadcasting. The average African station broadcasts its signals over a 100,000 square mile area, and in the Sudan, each station has approximately one million square miles to cover. This compares to an area of 1,600 square miles for the typical American transmitter. As a result, African radio broadcasters must be highly skilled if their listeners are to receive a strong, clear signal. They often lack information to accomplish this task, however. An adequate job of mapping the propagation of radio signals and studying ground conductivity in much of Africa has never been done. As a result, many African stations suffer from a scarcity of relevant data, insufficient transmission points, interference from powerful European stations, and inadequate spectrum allocation. African countries have objected to this, seeking a more equitable distribution of the radio spectrum.[6]

A comparison of radio, newspaper, and television technology as development media indicates that Third World countries should emphasize radio as the best means to reach the rural poor. It is cheap, simple, and flexible for creating multilingual programs which focus on development. It does not require an expensive infrastructure for distribution, excessively professional training, or sophisticated reception equipment, difficult to maintain. Moreover, radio broadcasting technology already exists in much of the Third World. What is needed is a commitment to use this media for development. Unfortunately, such a commitment seems to be lacking. UNESCO reports that in 85 countries, radio broadcasts in support of education and development average only five percent of all broadcast programming.[7]

In focusing on radio technology as the major development media, less developed countries must not neglect older methods of mass communication, however, less technical but very effective in many countries. Wall newspapers, posters, mimeographed leaflets, exhibitions, local fairs, music festivals, puppet shows, and traveling theater can also carry development messages. Media does not have to be technically sophisticated to be successful. It must be planned, however, applied in the interests of development and coordinated in such a way as to make information available to those who need it most--the rural poor.

POINT-TO-POINT INFORMATION TECHNOLOGY

In contrast to mass media, point-to-point communication is private in nature, composed primarily of two-way messages. It is no less essential to development, however. The management of production enterprises, the application of information to problem solving, the linkage of industry with markets and raw materials, the organization of political and social movements, and democratically oriented decision making all require adequate point-to-point communication. This can be facilitated by the combination of satellite and computer technology.

Satellites

Satellite technology has expanded rapidly during the past two decades as the following table demonstrates:

Table 4.1
Satellite system growth

Intelsat		
Year	Countries with antennas	Leased half-circuits
1965	5	150
1970	30	4,259
1975	71	13,369
1979	114	n.a.

Intersputnik		
Year	Countries with earth based stations	Satellite type
1973	3	Molnia-2 and
1975	6	Molnia-3
1979	9	Stationar
1980	12	Stationar

Sources: Intelsat Annual Report, 1979 and Documents from Intersputnik, 1979, reported in MacBride, Many Voices, One World, p. 62.

From 1957 to 1979, 2,100 satellites were launched. While more than two-thirds of those now in orbit are used for military purposes, satellites are also used for agriculture, aviation, banking, business, commerce, mining, meteorology, navigation, and entertainment.

There are 120 countries which have earth stations linked to satellites for communication; and in 1978, approximately 70 percent of one billion international telephone calls were placed via satellite.

Currently there are 33 communication satellite systems either functioning or under construction for national, regional, and international use. Many more are being planned. These satellite systems serve four types of uses:

1. International satellite systems: Two are presently in use. Intelsat enables its more than 100 member countries to communicate directly via satellite, and Intersputnik serves a similar function for socialist and some other states, although the Soviet communication satellites are primarily used for domestic communication.

2. Domestic and regional satellite systems: Examples are the USA's Westar, Comstar and RCA; the USSR's Molnia and Eckan, Canada's Anik and Indonesia's Palapa. Western Europe, the Middle East and Scandinavia will probably be the next areas to use regional satellites.

3. Marine and aeronautical satellite systems: These are mobile communication satellites, and examples include Marisat for ships and Aerosat (in planning) for airplanes.

4. Military satellites: These are used for communication, command and control as well as for various kinds of intelligence gathering and surveillance.[8]

The principle of communication by satellites has remained the same since American Telephone and Telegraph developed the first Telstar satellite in 1962. A ground transmitter sends a signal to the satellite which receives it, amplifies it, switches it to a different frequency then transmits it back to earth. However, each part of the system has been improved continually: the strength of the satellites' signals sent to the ground has increased; the satellites' coverage area and beam have been enlarged; the ability of the ground antenna and receiver to pick up signals has been strengthened; and the frequencies have been made more efficient. The need for greater power and better reception has been the motivating force behind the improvement of communication satellites.

Because of their weak signal, the first communication satellites could only link known, fixed points on the ground. They were classified according to ITU regulations as "Fixed Satellite Services" (FSS). They used the 4/6 GHz frequency band and required large and expensive ground receivers which were owned and operated mostly by national telecommunications agencies.

Intelsat and Intersputnik are the best examples of an FSS system. The former provides most of the world's satellite links for telephone, telex, data, and video. Like telephone signals in a terrestrial network, Intelsat's signals are not intended for public reception. The private nature of Intelsat's signals differentiate them clearly from those of broadcasting where public reception is the main purpose.

Domestic satellites in the United States also operate on the 4/6 GHz band in the ITU's fixed satellite service. Signals used by current Intelsat and United States Domsat systems can be received by much smaller antennas than the huge dishes, 30 meters in diameter, used by the earlier satellites. This has enabled cable television to operate more economically.

In the mid-1970s, the United States, Canada, and Japan led in the development of a second generation of experimental communication satellites which could use the 12/14 GHz frequency band. The Canadian Department of Communication and the United States National Aeronautics and Space Administration (NASA) launched the Hermes satellite for communication to remote communities in northern Canada. Canada's Telstar also developed the first of its Anik satellites, and Anik-B demonstrated that satellites were able to transmit television and radio programs direct to small antennas. In Japan two separate types of 12/14 GHz satellites were tested.[9] Most notable for less developed countries was NASA's ATS-6 satellite, used by India for the Satellite Instructional Television Experiment (SITE). This pioneered the use of satellite communication for development, so let's examine it more closely.

Satellite for Rural Development

During 1975-1976, India carried out a one-year pilot project which used a direct broadcast satellite for reaching remote villages with information about development. It provided an opportunity for India to deal with satellite television hardware, programming, budgeting, and management experimentally before launching its own satellite, and it presents us with an example of advanced information technology used for development.[10]

The United States through NASA loaned India four hours of satellite time each day, the Indian Space and Research Organization operated the ground stations, and All India Radio produced the television programs. Six underdeveloped, distant states were selected for the project, and community television sets were placed in 2,334 villages. Programs were video-taped in four languages, beamed to NASA's ATS-6 from the Ahmedabad earth station, and returned to receivers in the villages. In more densely populated regions, conventional television transmitters were used to redistribute the programs.

SITE's daily transmission time of four hours was divided between morning in-school broadcast and evening programming. Each morning 90 minutes were devoted to programs coinciding with the primary school curriculum. The evening's 150 minute broadcast was segmented into a 30 minute national program about news, public affairs, and national integration; and 120 minutes of regional programming with three 40 minute broadcasts in different languages for different regions. The programming content consisted of information supporting development projects in agriculture, health, and family planning (29 percent); entertainment related to local music, dance, and other forms of culture (25 percent); national awareness with information on Indian history, leaders, religion, and politics (33 percent), and dramas about social problems (10 percent).[11]

SITE's results indicate the advantages of satellite communication for otherwise unreachable rural areas. No sequential transmission lines were required, for the signal reached the ultimate receiver in a single "hop" via the satellite. Despite primitive conditions in the Indian countryside, the system was very reliable, rivalling western operations which are under much better conditions. At any one time, over 90 percent of the villages received the broadcast with excellent technical quality.

All India Radio produced imaginative programs on development which captured the attention of village people. Important information on agriculture, health and nutrition, indigenous culture, and public affairs was disseminated, and the programs always appeared on time.[12] For students, there were significant gains in language development and greater interest in learning. There seemed to be more student initiative, especially in science and language, among younger children. Attendance at school did not increase significantly, but that was probably the result of parents' rather than children's decisions.[13]

The satellite communication system provides another important advantage for rural development. It makes possible technically the creation of programs for a rural audience without first going through a stage of urban programming. As a result, programs can be based on rural rather than urban needs, establishing national television as a development media. Potentially there is a negative side to this, however. Satellite broadcasts can increase centralized programming and production, already a tendency within most countries. In India, centralized programming did permit broadcasting items of national concern, like news and public affairs, helping to integrate the country. There were a limited number of such programs, however, as India chose to lean toward a more regional approach.[14]

The main disadvantage is cost. SITE was an experimental, not a commercial, venture, with donated satellite time. Four hours of satellite time each day is very expensive, with the tariffs for India approximately $1,037 for the first ten minutes and $41.25 for each additional minute. This amounts to $10,525.50 per day, beyond the financial means of many poor countries. In fact, the average rates Asian countries pay for satellite transmission time is twice that of the United States and 60 to 70 percent higher than European tariffs. Moreover, much of the technology used in the SITE experiment, for example small earth stations, teleconferencing facilities, transportable terminals, and remote video origination, is either unavailable operationally or can be purchased only at a very high price.[15] The SITE project proved that less developed countries have the technical and programming ability to use and adapt advanced information technology. It will take considerable revenue, however, to make television an important development media in the Third World.

Telephones for the Countryside

Satellites can also be used for point-to-point communication involving telephony and telegraphy. This is made possible by launching a satellite in geosynchronous orbit at a height (22,282 miles at the peak ellipse) and speed sufficient to keep it essentially over one part of the earth as both rotate. These satellites can provide a viable alternative to conventional earth bound communication links. Moreover, the circuit costs per year of such a system could be substantially reduced if the satellite is designed to permit a large number of thin route (low traffic) circuits and inexpensive earth stations.

Technology is currently available to develop a system of thin-route rural telephony for a regional or global group of countries involving more than 10,000 earth stations. The size of this type of project would require sharing the space segment on a regional or group basis and realizing an economy of scale for the manufacture of ground hardware. Less developed countries could produce the ground equipment as part of their industrial development plan.

A satellite system offers some important advantages in point-to-point communication for the Third World. Generally, communication is more expensive for poor countries because the relatively small amount of traffic costs more per circuit than the developed states heavy traffic, which is trunked with many circuits to save material costs. The less developed countries would be helped by reducing the material costs of a thin route telephone system and coordinating national communications into a regional system providing service to a number of states. Satellite information technology can be useful in this process.

Satellite communication costs are unaffected by distance, so remote, rural locations can be served without cost disadvantage. Satellite telephone capacity can be installed on a need priority basis through adding earth stations which do not depend on the location of previous sites as do terrestrial links. This reduces total costs, because incremental expenses may be postponed until they are really needed. Radio and television signals as well as additional circuits may be added later, giving the system a flexibility not possible in terrestrial networks.[16] The satellite system is more reliable, more robust, and easier to maintain than a terrestrial system. Maintenance is simplified because the ground stations can be placed near settlements which are usually more accessible than earth bound telephone links.

With the expense of satellite circuits independent of distance and the cost of line-and-pole circuits nearly proportional to distance, there is a break even point beyond which satellite links become less expensive than terrestrial communication. The annual cost per circuit for a total telephone network depends on the range of lengths and the traffic demand. When the traffic is light and the distance great, as in rural areas, a satellite may be more economical. When the traffic is heavy and the distance small, as in an urban setting, terrestrial links are probably cheaper. These generalizations are conditioned, however, by local situations. For example, preexisting, earth bound facilities can eliminate the need for a ground station in a specific area. Therefore, a complete telephone network for both rural and urban service would require both satellite earth stations and terrestrial links in some combination. The satellite would supplement the earth bound system, not replace it; and the majority of a country's telephone traffic would probably still be earth bound, particularly in a small country with some urban areas of high traffic demand.[17] The satellite would also help link the less developed countries together. It permits direct, horizontal communication among Third World states, overcoming the present need to communicate through London, Paris, or New York. As a result, the satellite can reconnect more efficiently and economically the ancient communication links among many developing countries which were eroded during the colonial era.

There are two disadvantages with satellite telephony. The first involves initial capital outlay. A satellite using inexpensive circuits and ground stations is very costly, much more so than a satellite relying on more sophisticated and therefore more expensive ground stations and a higher level of traffic demand. No less developed country could afford the initial expenses of satellite, launch, and ground stations, nor could a poor country utilize the whole capacity at the outset. It is unlikely that a commercial satellite enterprise would find it profitable to develop such an expensive satellite specifically for rural use. However, a multinational consortium of developing countries might fund such an operation, if they were really committed to rural communication as a development goal.

The second disadvantage involves trust. A group of advanced countries might be persuaded to develop and launch a satellite, then lease it to the poor countries for rural telephony. That could lead to increased dependence, however, as more basic communication functions in the less developed countries pass through the foreign built satellite. If Third World leaders are disinclined to trust the advanced countries now, how could they tolerate mediated communication?

Technology has provided the possibility of using satellites for rural development, education, and point-to-point communications. This could help the less developed countries pursue economic, social, and political development, fulfill basic human needs in agriculture, health, and nutrition, integrate the societies, encourage participation, and bring Third World nations closer together. What is lacking is not technology. It is money and trust.

COMPUTERS AND INFORMATICS

The computer is a recent addition to information technology, and less developed countries can find many applications for computers in accomplishing their development objectives. Developing countries find it difficult to manage information, a characteristic of advanced industrial states. The computer is the most important tool for helping Third World nations in this process.

In the 1950s computers were experimental in nature. Electronic tubes were used to build large laboratory machines or commercial machines with limited use. With the invention of the transistor, however, it was possible to have large scale, reliable machines with reasonable power consumption, space requirements, and cost.

The 1960s were the "main frame" computer phase, where use was an elite activity with high purchasing and operating costs, beyond the means of developing countries. The common view at the time was that computers were a very expensive luxury. They were complex machines, requiring large initial capital outlay and high running costs due to the scarce expertise needed for operation. Time sharing naturally followed to expand the user base by giving simultaneous access to a central computational source. This provided better utilization for the expensive facility.

In the 1970s mini-computers were developed, and the computer experienced its "coming of age" phase. The availability of less expensive machines expanded their application to instrumentation, industrial automation, small business use, and office communication.[18]

The 1980s have already become the decade of information explosion because of four continuing, indeed accelerating, trends. One is an improved cost effectiveness ratio for the computer. Between 1955 and 1975, for example, the cost effeciveness ratio measured by the number of operations per second increased by 10^4 (10,000) times. A central memory of one million bytes, worth $1.5 million in 1969, was worth 100 times less by 1979, and the cost continues to decline.

A second trend is the miniaturization of hardware. One can now accommodate the equivalent of 50,000 transistors in a single chip costing $20. The density increase that we will have achieved by the year 2000 is likely to reach a figure of 10^8 (100 million) bits/mm^2, which is about 50,000 times the density we now have.

A third trend is the adaptation of software to user needs. As users moved from large systems to mini-computers and micro-processors, it became possible to use more simple programs, a part of the basic software being integrated into the hardware. As a result, the so-called advanced programming languages (Fortran, Cobol, and Algol) which date to the 1950s are being overtaken or at least joined by more "natural" languages that are similar to human speech patterns.

Finally, the parallel and complementary process of computers and telecommunications, called telematics, permits network building. The first networks were effected by earth bound links and limited to one enterprise or one professional sector like banking, insurance, or airlines.[19] More recently, computers have been linked more closely to permit greater flexibility. Multiple terminals in a star-like configuration permit various forms of teleprocessing, the interlinking of computers for data transmission, and the bringing together of data bases, process, storage, and filing functions for customized data processing services.

The communication satellite has made it possible to establish integrated information networks at national and international levels, for the communication of data via satellite is independent of distance in terms of transmission time and cost. This new form of communication is called informatics, defined as: "the new scien-

tific, technological and engineering disciplines related
to computers in information handling and processing,
management, automation, communication and other fields;
and its wider social, economic and cultural aspects."[20]

Informatics has become an important industry to
advanced, industrial states where nearly one-half the
work force is employed in the information and
communication sector. Much of this industry involves
network information services (NIS), the transmission of
data through circuits. These services were developed by
the United States, Japan and Western Europe in the early
1970s and use existing telephone switching networks,
telex networks, and leased circuits for communication.
The sale of data through NIS in 1980 totaled an
estimated $3,000 million, comprising one-third of all
computer industry revenue. The Western European market
for NIS was approximately $1,360 million in 1980, up
from $410 million in 1975.[21] For the United States,
informatics is a vital new enterprise. A Department of
State report clearly defines the American interest:

> "The United States has national security,
> political, ideological, economic and technolo-
> gical stakes. ... Our national security is
> dependent on advanced telecommunication
> systems. Politically we are committed to a
> broad exchange of information both domes-
> tically and internationally.

> "Our economic interest is obvious: Our indus-
> trial base relies on adequate communication;
> large corporations have become increasingly
> dependent on world-wide computer circuits.
> Moreover, the United States is the world's
> largest producer and consumer of telecommuni-
> cations equipment and services (exports of
> communication, computer and auxiliary hardware
> exceed $5 billion per year).

> "Technologically, the United States holds a
> lead in most areas of satellite communication,
> in fiber optic communication (along with
> Japan) and in very large switching systems.
> In other areas of basic communication technol-
> ogy such as microwave transmission systems or
> satellite earth stations, the United States,
> Japan and Western Europe are roughly equiva-
> lent technologically. In computer and data
> communication and in their application, the
> United States is commercially dominant."[22]

Improvements in computers and satellites have created a
new industry for advanced countries and led to an explosion in the world's volume of information. This has

resulted in a change that must be considered qualitative, and it will affect all aspects of human activity.

Informatics is also important for less developed countries. This was recognized as early as 1971 with a UNESCO resolution:

> During the second United Nations Development Decade, the application of science and technology should make a vital contribution to the economic and social advancement of all countries, particularly the developing countries; and ... computer technology is destined to play a leading role.[23]

In the past it was thought that telecommunications and computers were too advanced for less developed countries, that they follow industrial development rather than precede it. Now there is the realization; that informatics is more a precondition than a consequence of development. Unfortunately, Third World countries still have little access to informatics technology. Ten years after the United Nations resolution, approximately 95 percent of the world's computer capacity, measured in equipment value is in advanced industrial states. These rich countries invested $16.60 per capita on computers in 1965, and increased this to $54.40 in 1977. The poor countries invested only $1.60 per capita in 1968 and $6.70 in 1977. As with so many other indicators, there is a large informatics disparity between advanced and less developed countries.[24]

Informatics provides two advantages for the developing countries. The first is increased cost effectiveness in using the computer, already discussed above. What other technological resource has actually decreased in price over the last decade? The low cost and small size of new systems make them affordable for even the poorest countries, although satellite links are still quite expensive. The other advantage is the computer's flexibility. It can be used for a wide variety of purposes relating to development. One use involves data bases, magnetic memories capable of representing billions of words, each available rapidly from the computer system.

Data bases have proved useful in numerous ways. In India, for example, the government created the National Informatics Center to provide an integrated data base for government planning. Like other less developed countries, India's economy includes agriculture, energy, and basic industry. For agriculture, climate variations, geographical differences in geological and hydrological structures require diverse crops and highly decentralized land holdings. To plan and monitor India's agriculture, a data base was constructed and is used to model conditions involving water, climate, soil,

fertilizer, grain collection and distribution, and livestock.

Industry in India is based on a system of licenses
which monitor the expenditure of foreign exchange, promote an equitable distribution of industries throughout
the country, prevent monopolization, and coordinate the
indigenous development and foreign purchase of technology. This is a very complicated procedure for a
country the size of India, so a data base is currently
being constucted through the National Information Center
to organize the license monitoring process.

There is also an Indian data base for energy which
helps plan and monitor efficient use. The energy sector
is directly related to agriculture, because the economy
is agriculturally based, and it plays an important part
in determining the overall growth rate. Subsoil water
exploitation depends on cheap electricity and its
distribution over a vast rural area. The available
electric power is widely scattered, however, with coal
in the east and hydroelectric power in the far north and
the south, influenced by rainfall. Indian planners need
to reach a balance among power generated from coal,
hydro, and nuclear plants, and the computer monitors
power demand and supply to reach the most efficient mix
of generation and distribution.[25]

Other less developed countries are also using
informatics. In Malaysia, a monitoring system using a
data base keeps track of 20,000 development projects
throughout the country. On-line terminals permit
administrators to review the status of projects and take
action when necessary. An African country uses a computer for scheduling debt payment. Due to increased efficiency, the payments are made on time, realizing a discount from suppliers. Another nation uses a computer to
project cash flow for public works projects. This has
improved cash flow to a point that money is available to
finance other projects, increasing employment. Computers are also used for financial accounting and
budgeting, personnel records and administrative procedures, land reform monitoring, housing, employment, and
epidemiology studies to improve public health.[26]

One of the most flexible uses for computers in less
developed countries is for teaching, facilitiated by
miniaturization and decreased costs. Students can use
the computer to learn at their own pace, receive
specialized instruction adapted to their own needs, and
simulate experiments. There is a shortage of trained
teachers in the Third World. When the computer is used
for "drill and practice," the teacher is free for other
duties and the number of children receiving education
can be increased.

For monitoring resources, microwave applications
have been used. The remote sensing of the earth by
satellite and analysis of the results by computer

permits advanced weather prediction, land use planning, pollution monitoring, agricultural crop forecasts, forest inventories, soil erosion prevention, and discovery of water resources.

Finally, informatics can establish communication networks which go far beyond the links associated with traditional forms of point-to-point communication. Decentralized groups can be brought together with communication made horizontal, localized, diversified. This promotes integration, fosters the building of interest groups, and facilitates greater popular participation. Flexibility, adaptability, and low cost are major advantages informatics technology provides less developed countries.

There are disadvantages, however, in the use of informatics. First, the cost of computers has dropped substantially, but the transmission costs of data via satellite are still very expensive. Moreover, using foreign data bases can be risky. The foreign country could interfere with the satellite transmission by destroying an operational development plan which requires the data. Less developed countries may find it more economical and safer to develop their own data bases, as India has done, perhaps through multinational cooperation.

A second disadvantage involves privacy, personal freedom, and civil liberties. Information can refine the practice of domestic surveillance--eavesdropping and wire tapping--thereby systematically violating human rights. It's quite easy to monitor telephone calls using highly automated equipment. Telephone numbers of political undesirables and dissidents can be programmed into the computer, their conversations taped and recorded. The computer can also be used to keep personnel dossiers on political opponents, a use that is probably made of an IBM computer by DINA, Chile's secret police.[27]

Third, there may be nothing inherently political about a computer, but the lack of indigenous talent in science, engineering, and technology often means that western advisors become part of the transfer of technology, increasing a poor country's dependence. Moreover, informatics is not culturally neutral. It reflects a certain way of thinking and a certain social and economic organization. It is the product of a rationalist, western culture. Once such a system is installed, it becomes an enduring cultural artifact, changing the way its users perceive the world and their own culture.

Finally, one must candidly give warning about the potential boredom and sterility of the information society. The post office clerk who reads zip codes from envelopes all day and key punches the data into a machine that prints directions to a sorter is typical of sacrificed human potential. Less developed countries must find a way to get maximum use out of informatics without making people homogenous, depersonalizing them or destroying their values and their culture.

INTERNATIONAL ISSUES

If a less developed country chooses to use broadcasting, satellites, and computers for development, its decision makers need to be aware of certain international issues associated with these information technologies. As a user of the technology, the Third World country will want to safeguard its national interests by taking informed and responsible positions. The two most important international issues related to these technologies are information commerce (data flows)[28] and regulations.

Data Flows and Information Commerce

Many years ago, the first acts of war often involved a blockade to close transportation and communication. Presently, the prelude to war often involves the closing of airports. During a coup or a revolution, a major target is often the radio and television stations to permit the new regime communication with its citizens and with other countries. Information commerce, the transmission of data via satellites, cannot so easily be controlled, and it has become an important international issue.[29] It is also a complicated one, with states arguing for and against the control of information flows in the form of data, films, news, and books. There are many sub-issues in this discussion, but the three most important to the less developed country involved with information technology are data flows through remote earth sensing, telematics, and satellite broadcasting.

Currently NASA's Landsat satellites can collect data about a country's resources without that country knowing it by passive microwave sensing. Information about oil deposits, crop yields, or mineral concentrations are valuable to corporations as well as to developing countries.[30] The former can use the data to make better judgments about their investments at the expense of the Third World state. With such data, for example, mining companies could take low-cost options on land before a government realizes that the land is quite valuable. This seems unfair to many in the Third World, but it is viewed as good business practice by transnational corporations and the earned reward of technological research and development by advanced states.

International law grants a country exclusive rights

over its national resources, by custom, and United
Nations Resolution 626 (VII) declares, without the authority of law: No country may "impede the exercise of
sovereignty of any state over its national resources."
What is not clear, however, is whether or not a country
can exercise exclusive rights to <u>data</u> about its resources. Presently, any party can purchase at low cost
data collected from Landsat remote microwave sensing.
For an additional, larger charge, the data will be
analyzed and interpreted. Once this has occurred,
however, it becomes proprietary information, and therefore private. Many less developed countries do not have
the technical resources to analyze and use the raw data,
so they are dependent on advanced states for information
about their own resources, a most uneasy position.

To many Third World states, this is an issue of
national sovereignty. Not trusting the advanced countries, they would prefer to have remote sensing regulated by an international body, like the United Nations,
rather than controlled by the United States government
and transnational corporations. The Americans reject
this notion, arguing that the flow of information should
not be hindered by national borders or international
organizations. The issue continues to be a problem, and
less developed countries using information technology
are understandably concerned.

Telematics, the transmission of computer data cross
borders, also involves national sovereignty. In the
information age, international political borders are no
longer clearly delineated. Balkan Bulgarian Airlines,
Malev Hungarian Airlines, and Lot Polish Airlines, among
others, have made reservations for local flights through
a computer in Atlanta, Georgia. The loading and unload-
ing of Norwegian freighters, oil shipments from the Per-
sian Gulf, and the production of auto parts in Canada
are arranged by foreign computers. Who controls these
information resources? By what means? In whose
national interests? These questions were asked in the
mid-1970s by Harvard's Project on Information Resources,
but the answers are still not clear.[31]

The processing of much European data is done by
American computers which receive the data via satellite
transmission or cable. In fact, approximately 90
percent of the records held in data banks are estimated
to exist in the United States. Often this data is about
individuals, dealing with their banking, insurance, or
credit. European governments have become concerned over
their inability to protect their citizens' privacy when
the information is transferred to foreign computers. As
a result, Germany and Sweden have strengthened their
privacy laws. The French have established a government
commission to study this international information commerce, and Canada has issued a report, <u>Telecommunica-
tions in Canada</u>, that recommends greater national

independence in computer services.[32]

Louis Joinet expressed his concern at a symposium on transborder data flows sponsored by The Organization of Economic Cooperation and Development:

> Information is power and economic information is economic power. Information has an economic value, and the ability to store and process certain types of data may well give one country political and technological advantage over other countries. This, in turn, leads to a loss of national sovereignty ...[33]

In response, the EEC established EURONET, a consortium of nine countries' computer interests to develop European held data bases. The purpose is both political and economic. They want to keep control over European information while they stimulate the growth of their domestic computer industries.

Until recently, this was an issue for developed states alone. As more less developed countries use informatics, relying more heavily on computers and data bases, however, it will concern them also. Many African countries already use French computers to store and process banking and credit data. The same information needed for development planning can be used by marketing specialists and advertisers to change consumer spending patterns in less developed countries. This should concern decision makers who want to encourage saving for the creation of development capital rather than spending on consumer goods. Transborder computer data flow is an issue of international information commerce that will become more important, and discussions will continue at international organizations. Decision makers choosing this information technology will want to think carefully about a position that will protect their sovereignty and their citizens' privacy.

Direct broadcasts from satellites (DBS) is another kind of data flow which has been widely debated. As the SITE project in India demonstrated, DBS can be more flexible, more sturdy, and more efficient than conventional ground transmitters. With international cooperation, DBS could provide greater diversity in programming, more uses for television, even two-way video communication across borders. However, many Third World countries have been joined by the Soviet Union and other countries to denounce direct broadcasting without prior consent. (Canada and Sweden want programming participation by the receiving countries as well.) Some reject the advertising that would probably accompany DBS. Others fear the power of television to invade their cultures and destroy their values. Many seek strong regulations, and the Soviets have even claimed the right to destroy any foreign satellite broadcasting within their borders, presumably with a "killer satellite." The United States position is against regulation as politically unwise and technically premature. Regulation at this time might inhibit technical innovation and limit a country's right to use DBS within its own borders.

In fact, DBS across national frontiers is not so serious a problem. Any state not wanting to receive the satellite's signals could prevent the use of antenna dishes and the electronic components required for reception. DBS may have become an issue for debate as a symbol for expressing fears about cultural invasion.[34]

These problems involve national sovereignty and economic growth. Many developing countries view remote earth sensing without permission as a violation of their national sovereignty and an intrusion into their rights of resource management. They particularly resent the classification of analyzed data as proprietary, giving the transnational corporations greater advantage in relations with the Third World. The transmission of computer data across borders also affects sovereignty and economics, making the less developed countries dependent on advanced states for analysis of the very information they seek to use in achieving self-reliance. What is worse, some fear that information can be used to undermine their development plans through marketing research promoting consumption. There is little the less developed countries can do presently about these two types of data flow, but they can strenuously protest the signal flow of DBS as a potential threat both to sovereignty and to culture. There are other ways, as well, that the developing countries are exerting themselves and demanding protection of their interests in exchange for cooperating on international regulations.

International Regulations

Use of the electro-magnetic spectrum and the geosynchronous orbit are two issues where international cooperation and regulations are essential. These resources are supranational, phenomena of nature which are the common property of humankind. They are regulated by the ITU through its World Administrative Radio Conferences (WARC) where the less developed countries have recently been demanding greater equity.[35]

The spectrum is the total range of possible rates at which electro-magnetic energy oscillates. All energy travels at the same speed (180,000 miles per second), but electro-magnetic energy oscillates like waves at different frequencies and different wave lengths. Frequency means the number of waves per second which pass a point, while wave lengths mean the distance between one wave crest and the next. The larger the wave length, the shorter the frequency; the shorter the wave length, the higher the frequency. Signals are imposed on the radio waves, so higher frequencies (shorter wave lengths) carry more signals than lower ones. One wave length or cycle each second is a hertz, the basic unit of measurement. One thousand cycles is a kilohertz; one million a megahertz and one thousand million a gigahertz. Radio frequencies range between ten kilohertz to 300 gigahertz.[36]

Various communication devices use up parts of the spectrum at different rates. For example, one color television channel requires a bandwidth of six MHz. The same six MHz bandwidth could also transmit 40 FM radio channels or over 3,000 telephone calls. The entire very low frequency (VLF) band could transmit one-three-hundredth of a television channel, low frequency (LF) one-twentieth, medium frequency (MF) half of one television channel. The high frequency (HF) band could transmit four television channels, very high frequency (VHF) 45, ultra high frequency (UHF) 450, and super high frequency (SHF) 4,500. Extra high frequency (EHF) could accommodate as many as 34,000 color television channels.[37]

The available frequencies seem large, but they are in heavy demand, limited by nature and regulated by the ITU. It takes careful management to avoid wasting this precious resource. The spectrum has been divided into 20 parts or bands which carry specific services such as radio and television programs, mobile radio, radio-astronomy, satellite broadcasts, data transfers, remote earth sensing and others. All users must cooperate to share frequencies regarding time, geography, and strength of signal to avoid interference and optimize maximum efficient use.[38]

There is particularly great demand for high frequency (HF) service, and it is currently being over used. The Voice of America, the British Broadcasting Company, Radio Beijing, Radio Moscow and other international broadcasters favor HF, and there has been heavy HF demand in the west for mobile telephones and "beepers" to keep in touch with one's office or home. Earlier allocations of the band for fixed rather than broadcast use have been abandoned, but many advanced countries, including the United States, have not given up their no longer used allocations. Less developed countries have become heavy users of the HF band for radio broadcasting, police work, and the encouragement of social activities in remote, rural areas. It is a particularly useful means to reach their dispersed population without having to construct many expensive transmitters. Moreover, radios using the HF band tend to be less expensive than other kinds of equipment.[39]

Bandwidths can be used more efficiently by

employing advanced technology both in sending and receiving signals. Generally, the more modern the communication technology, the more efficiently it uses its assigned bandwidth of the spectrum. Developed countries with more advanced equipment can "stretch" their share of the spectrum bandwidth through technological innovation. They adapt receivers to protect against interference, use more accurate directional antennas, and reduce a channel's bandwidth through a sophisticated technique called "single sideband" transmission. Poor countries have older, cheaper, more primitive equipment. They can't afford the west's sophisticated hardware and "waste" parts of the spectrum with their outdated equipment.[40]

In the past, WARC has allocated bands on a "first come, first served" or "squatter's rights" basis. Countries which had the advanced technology to use more of the spectrum were permitted to do so because it was believed that new technologies would be found to "stretch" further the spectrum bandwidths. At the 1979 WARC, however, the less developed countries voted to have frequencies allocated to them in the gigahertz band used for satellite broadcasting, despite their lack of satellites. The United States almost refused to cooperate with this decision, seriously considering the entry of a reservation. The conference finally decided that less developed countries should have more equitable access to frequencies and that developed states should "clean up the master registry," by relinquishing their unused frequencies.[41] This was a major change in policy for WARC and a political victory for Third World countries. Advanced states viewed the conference and its decision as an issue of technological planning. Less developed countries saw it in terms of justice and equity.

Third World countries are also demanding reservation of the geosynchronous orbit for their later use. Like the spectrum, this orbit is a supranational phenomena, limited by nature. At 22,282 miles peak ellipse and the speed of the earth's rotation, a satellite in this orbit can "park" in one spot over land or sea for permanent communication. So many satellites have been launched into the orbit, however, that it is becoming crowded. The less developed countries want space reserved for their geosynchronous satellites when they are ready to go into space. Western countries oppose this, claiming that the "first come, first served," "squatter's rights" principle is best and that new technology will ultimately expand capacity. This argument was not settled at the 1979 WARC. Rather it was postponed until later conferences when the less developed countries will no doubt pursue it further.

These are obviously political rather than simply technical issues. Information commerce and the

international regulation of the spectrum and
geosynchronous orbit are areas in which the less
developed countries seek to exert power, and
international organizations must recognize their
interests in a spirit of justice, fairness, and equity.
Without cooperation, the use of these information
resources will be threatened not only for Third World
states, but for advanced countries as well.

Information technology in broadcasting, computers,
and satellites can be important development tools,
permitting less developed countries to manage information and resources, communicate with their citizens and
with each other, and support an overall development
plan. How effectively Third World countries use information technology to promote humane development depends
both on regional and international cooperation as well
as the values each developing state seeks to foster.

NOTES

1. MacBride, pp. 124-27, using statistics from
Communication Policy in Brazil (New York: UNESCO, 1975) and
UNESCO Statistical Yearbook 1977 (Paris: UNESCO, 1977). It must
be noted that newspapers pass through many more hands in
developing countries than in advanced ones.

2. Smith, pp. 48-49 and "A Glimpse into Communication
Statistics," Research paper number 6, The International
Commission for the Study of Communication Problems, on file at
UNESCO headquarters, Paris and the Institute of International
Communication, London.

3. High costs due to the world-wide shortage of newsprint
may be overcome by the cultivation of kenaf, a fibrous plant
which offers a potential substitute for wood in the production of
newsprint.

4. MacBride, pp. 61-62, 215-16.

5. Ibid.

6. Smith, pp. 50-51.

7. Reported in Jonathan F. Gunter, The United States and
the Debate on the World "Information Order" (Washington, D.C.:
Academy for Educational Development, Inc., 1979), p. 87, based on
1974 data.

8. MacBride, pp. 63-64.

9. John Howkins, "The Next Wave of Television," Intermedia,
vol. 9, no. 4 (July 1981), pp. 14-15.

10. India's attempt to launch an operational satellite in
1982 failed when the rocket carrying the satellite exploded in
flight. In August 1983 the United States' space shuttle
"Challenger" launched the $50 million Insat 1-B satellite for
India at a service cost of $14 million.

11. Bella Mody, "Programming for SITE," Journal of Communication, vol. 29, no. 4 (Autumn 1979), pp. 90-98.

12. Clifford Block, Dennis R. Foote and John K. Mayo, "SITE Unseen: Implications for Programming and Policy," Journal of Communication, vol. 29, no. 4 (Autumn 1979), p. 115.

13. Sneklate Shukla, "The Impact of SITE on Primary School Children," Journal of Communication, vol. 29, no. 4 (Autumn 1979), pp. 99-105.

14. Block, et al., p. 119.

15. "Asia's Special Need for Satellite Links," Intermedia, vol. 9, no. 4 (July 1981), p. 87 and Anna Casey-Stahmer, "The Era of Experimental Satellites: Where Do We Go From Here?," Journal of Communication, vol. 29, no. 4 (Autumn 1979), p. 141.

16. Heather E. Hudson, "Implications for Development Communications," Journal of Communication, vol. 29, no. 1 (Winter 1979), pp. 182-83.

17. Ronald E. Rice and Edwin B. Parker, "Telecommunication Alternatives for Developing Countries," Journal of Communication, vol. 29, no. 4 (Autumn 1979), pp. 125-26.

18. Yakup Parker, "Informatics and Development: UNESCO's Approach for the 1980's," in Computers in Developing Nations, J.M. Bennett and R.E. Kalman, editors (Amsterdam: North Holland Publishing Company, 1981), pp. 12-13.

19. Oliver Rateau, "Informatics: Evolution and Use in the 1980's, with Particular Reference to Developing Countries" in Bennett and Kalman, p. 5.

20. Yakup Parker, p. 11. The New English word "informatics" comes from the French informatique. A new English word was required, because the term "computer science" is too narrowly technical in its connotation.

21. MacBride, pp. 78-79.

22. United States Department of State, Report Submitted to Congress Pursuant to the Foreign Relations Authorization Act Fiscal Year 1979, Public Law 95-426 (Washington: Government Printing Office, March 1979), pp. 67-83.

23. United Nations Economic and Social Council, "International Cooperation with a View to the Use of Computers and Computational Techniques for Development," E/RES/1571(L), May 1971, p. 1.

24. MacBride, pp. 129-30.

25. B. Nag, "Appropriate Computerization--An Instrument of Development and Social Change in Developing Countries" in Bennett and Kalman, p. 54.

26. Ismail B. Sulaiman, "Computers in Developing Countries: Malaysia's Experience," in Bennett and Kalman, pp. 237-42.

27. M.U. Porat, "Global Implications of the Information Society," Journal of Communication, vol. 28, no. 1 (Winter 1978), p. 76.

28. The phrase "transborder data flow" should be avoided, according to Philippe Lemoine, a consultant to "Le Chef de la Mission à L'Informatique" of France because it "gives the impression of being a problem which is still technical and obscure. ... To be more precise as to its potency in levels of employment and ... balance of payments, a simpler term would be

international information commerce." Phillipe Lemoine in
Systemes d'Informatique (May 1979), a magazine of CII-Honeywell
Bull.

29. John Howkins, "The Next Wave of Television," p. 17.

30. Tina Thompson, "Get the Picture?," TRW Systems and
Energy Magazine, vol. 5, no. 1 (Winter 1981), pp. 12-17.

31. Information Resources Policy Annual Report, vol. 2
(Cambridge, Mass.: Harvard University Project on Information and
Resources, 1976), p. 8.

32. Telecommunications in Canada (Ottawa: National
Parliament of Canada, Consultative Committee Report, April 1979),
pp. 63-65.

33. Louis Joinet in an address to the OECD symposium on
"transborder data flows and the protection of privacy," Vienna,
Austria, September 1977 quoted in G. Russel Pipes, "National
Policies, International Debates," Journal of Communication, vol.
29, no. 3 (Summer 1979), pp. 114-23.

34. Gunter, pp. 96-97.

35. Created by the Madrid Telecommunications Convention of
1932, the International Telecommunications Union controls all
varieties of telecommunications. With its central office in
Berne, Switzerland, the union governs according to the 1949
Telecommunications Convention and its subsequent amendments.

36. Smith, pp. 117-18.

37. John Howkins, "What is the World Administrative Radio
Conference?," Journal of Communication, vol. 29, no. 1 (Winter
1979), pp. 144-49.

38. John Howkins, "The Management of the Spectrum,"
Intermedia, vol. 7, no. 5 (September 1979), pp. 10-22.

39. Hudson, pp. 179-86.

40. Gunter, p. 40.

41. Smith, pp. 122-24. For a detailed account of the 1979
World Administrative Radio Conference, see the New York Times,
September 23, 25, 28, 29, November 10, 17, 22, 24, 25 and
December 4, 1979.

5
Communication Values: Democracy, Freedom, and Responsibility

> All rights tends to declare themselves absolute to their logical extreme. Yet all in fact are limited by the neighborhood of principles ... other than those on which the particular right is founded, and which become strong enough to hold their own when a certain point is reached.
>
> Oliver Wendell Holmes

> Freedom of expression is not our only liberty. ... It is entitled to no imperium; it must democratically live with other guarantees and rights.
>
> Charles Rembar

> The objectives of the press: to understand the popular feeling and give expression to it; ... to arouse among the people certain desirable sentiments; ...fearlessly to expose popular defects.
>
> Mahatma Gandhi

During the nineteenth and early twentieth centuries, a European country acquired some of the world's most sophisticated means of communication including numerous daily newspapers, a first rate film industry, magazine and book publishing, large international news agencies, and a radio network which reached the whole nation. The country established one of Europe's best point-to-point communication systems using radio, telephone, and telegraph as well as road, rail, and air connections which were the envy of its neighbors. Scientific research and development combined with advanced production facilities for communication equipment helped the nation develop self-reliance and emerge as a global political and economic leader.

This country did not achieve humane development,

however. Lacking the values of freedom, democracy, and responsibility, it became a notorious aggressor, enslaving and killing millions and pushing humanity into global warfare. Without communication values, the technological means to communicate gave Adolf Hitler powerful tools of domination through propaganda, and Germany suffered its Götterdämmerung.

Today, with careful planning, international cooperation and a better understanding of development goals, less developed countries can acquire the means to communicate and use information technology for productive ends. They may do so while establishing self-reliance through choosing appropriate technology, adapting it to their specific needs, and sharing research and development for indigenous technology with other Third World states. They may also be successful in changing international communication policies regarding spectrum frequency allocations, the geosynchronous orbit, and the flow of data across borders. All this is not enough, however, for the less developed countries to attain a genuinely humane form of development.

Mass media and point-to-point information technology do not guarantee participatory communication, nor do they automatically lead to greater democracy. More is needed if economic, social, and political development are to achieve humane goals. To be just, a productive and efficient economic system requires participatory management and workers' rights. To attain equality, social development demands the integration of all citizens into their society, attention to their welfare, and respect for their divergent cultures and life styles. To acquire legitimacy and support, political development requires rights to independent thought, freedom of expression, participation in public affairs, and non-violent opposition to authority. Communication and information technology can assist in the process of humane development only if certain values are present, particularly among the elite who hold power. This chapter examines three of these values--democratic communication, freedom to communicate, and journalist responsibility.

DEMOCRATIC COMMUNICATION

The world is composed of many different types of government, some authoritarian, some democratic, although no country has achieved complete democracy. Nevertheless, this is an age in which the democratic ideal is widely shared, an era when most governments at least claim authority on the principle of popular will. Communication shares this ideal, seeking to serve people and respond to their needs. Despite the failure to achieve full democracy either in government or in communication, the principle of democracy is an important human value which must be encouraged.

Democratic communication is an evolutionary process, changing over time and achieving varying levels in different states. It aims, however, at a goal which makes communication more responsive to popular will, more attuned to humane development. Democratization in communication may be defined as a process in which "a) the individual becomes an active partner and not a mere object of communication; b) the variety of messages exchanged increases; and c) the extent and quality of social representation or participation in communication are augmented."[1]

It is a process which is basic to the human condition. To communicate is to be human, and human beings have an innate need to exchange information, feelings, and ideas. Few would question the need to communicate if this were a society based solely on interpersonal, oral communication. It is the intervention of technology in the communication process which raises questions about this basic need to communicate, but machines should not change people's essential needs.

The same need is shared by societies, groups of individuals which developed bonds through communication. To deny a society or a nation the exchange of information or self-expression is inhuman. It destroys the personality and culture of the society and makes all humankind poorer. The need to communicate is thus shared by all people and all nations. Without it, human beings are denied their essence, their basic civilized needs.

A number of forces are at work in the evolution of this need. One is individuals' desire to communicate with others, impelling them to form a society and come together for cultural, economic, and political ends. Another force is society's will to express itself, resulting in more complex forms of communication through information technology which leads to even more extended social structure. The convergence of these two forces have led to a tension of values and conflict, complicating the emergence of a recognized right to communicate.

During a distant, primitive past when communication was interpersonal, freedom of opinion emerged as an individual right. People began to believe that others had the right to their own opinion, even when they disagreed with accepted ideas. In opposition to this emerging right were religious, social, and political forces which sought orthodoxy through inquisition and persecution. The right to freedom of opinion grew, however, despite repression. During the Renaissance and the Reformation, it was a demand which challenged social authority, and it is the first expression of the right to communicate.

With the invention and increased use of printing came additional demands for the right of free expression. The printing press provided the means to reach large numbers of people. Consequently, individuals sought to use this media to express themselves even when they disagreed with church, state, or society. It took many centuries, but freedom of expression was gradually accepted and recognized in the first Declaration of the Rights of Man.

Freedom of the press was the next demand made by individuals to social and political authority. It was the result of new information technology which led to mass circulation newspapers and reflected the desire of individuals to oppose with words and ideas injustice and arbitrary rule. Like the other rights, this one was not accepted without struggle. It was opposed by kings, clerics, and colonialists, but freedom of the press was recognized in the new world by the Constitution of the United States and in France by the National Law of 1881. In much of the world, this right is still denied, but its power is manifest by the extent to which authoritarian governments try to rationalize their censorship. The invention of more sophisticated forms of mass media such as radio, television, film and their use in propaganda during World War II led to the proclamation in 1948 of a more extensive right "to seek, receive and impart information and ideas through any media and regardless of frontiers."[2]

A further step is necessary if individuals are to succeed in their struggle with social authority. The right to communicate is the next demand. Voiced in many countries, it is the cumulation of opinion, expression, press, and information rights. It builds on these earlier rights, extending them to encompass a more complete expression of human dignity. Without the right to communicate, democracy can never be fully realized.[3]

The right to communicate is not yet a completely developed concept. In 1974, Sweden introduced a resolution at a UNESCO conference instructing the Director General to examine how more active participation in the communication process might be possible and to analyze the right to communicate.[4] Subsequently, the International Commission for the Study of Communications Problems put the right to communicate on its agenda as a major item. In 1982, a Conference in Bucharest, Rumania was held to examine this right further. It has been under discussion at the International Institute of Communication (London) and at a number of universities in different countries.

A possible formulation of this right is:

> Everyone has the right to communicate: the components of this comprehensive human right include but are not limited to the following specific communication rights:
>
> a) a right to assembly, a right to discuss, a right to participate and related <u>association</u> rights;
> b) a right to inquire, a right to be informed, a right to inform and related <u>information</u> rights; and
> c) a right to culture, a right to choose, a right to privacy, and related <u>development</u> rights.[5]

Let's examine these three elements--association, information, and development to understand democratic communication more fully.

The need for communication to be participatory is central to greater democracy in the exchange of messages. Domestically, interactive or two-way communication is necessary if the process of communication is to be more than simply the dissemination of information from the elite to the mass. Internationally, participation in communication involves access to existing facilities. This includes equitable use of satellite systems, data banks, spectrum frequencies, and the geosynchronous orbit. There must also be participation in the policy planning process of international communication by all states, advanced as well as developing. This requires input into the decision making process of international organizations such as the International Telecommunications Union and UNESCO (which already exists) as well as participation in private organizations such as transnational corporations, news agencies, film and television production and distribution companies. Moreover, all countries should share in the creation of international media content. This could be realized through more consultation on program content and greater efforts to exchange programming between advanced and less developed countries, with Third World programming appearing in the western media. This is difficult, given the commercial nature of American networks and programming. However, public broadcasting in the United States and the increased use of cable television makes an effort at this kind of participation more feasible.

Associational rights aimed at greater participation are vital to the development of better international understanding and the creation of new ideas. An example of this process is expression of the right to communicate itself, which 'springs from multi-cultural exchanges. Participation is essential for the illiterate and poor who have no access to information except through oral, interpersonal communication. The world will better understand their needs and put them on its agenda only when their governments achieve associational representation in international communication.

Information rights, the second element, has been discussed more widely. Article 19 of the Universal Declaration of Human Rights claims that everyone has the right to "seek, receive and impart information;" but this claim has not been realized. Thus far, it has been treated as an information receiver's right in which mass media have provided a one-way flow of information with few sources and many receivers. In the future, the right to information must be more active with the receivers indicating what information they need by means of two-way communication and feedback.[6] They must be free to interview official and nonofficial sources and transmit their reports without government interference. Restrictions on journalists' access, their ability to visit countries, or areas within countries are clearly in conflict with information rights.[7]

The third area, development rights, involves cultural evolution. It is the least sharply defined, the newest area of communication rights arising from charges of cultural domination. It includes the right to be left alone in privacy, permitting a culture to develop its own values without interference from outside. It also means respect for the languages and cultures of smaller countries and minorities within larger countries. In short, development rights mean that "everyone has the right not to communicate."[8]

The pursuit of association, information, and development rights would go a long way toward the establishment of the right to communicate and with it greater democracy in communication. It would provide greater participation in the process of international communication, a genuinely free flow of information rather than the current one-way flow, and the protection of cultural diversity. There are many obstacles, however, in establishing the right to communicate as a practical, effective principle.

One such problem involves differing interpretations of the right to communicate, particularly the right to exchange information. An example of these differences is Soviet and American views of the Helsinki Accord, the Final Act of the Conference on Security and Cooperation in Europe. Western states interpret the so called "third basket" of the accord as a victory for the free flow of ideas because it calls for increased human contacts and more information exchange. The Soviet Union and East European states emphasize other parts of the document, reaffirming national sovereignty, and argue that they have a right to restrict information which they find offensive. When dissident groups were formed in the Soviet Union and Czechoslovakia to monitor adherence to the human rights aspects of the Helskinki Accord, western journalists sought to contact these groups and report their complaints. The west claims that its journalists have a right to cover the dissidents, based on the Helsinki Accord, while the Soviets argue that such coverage would restrict the government's right to maintain domestic order. Based on this principle of national sovereignty, eastern states feel justified in continuing their restrictive information policies, and some less developed countries are pursuing a similar path.[9]

This reflects a fundamental conceptual difference about the nature of the state. In some countries where successful struggles have limited royal prerogatives over individuals, freedom of information and opinion are considered essential to the functioning of democracy, for they permit government power to be controlled. In other countries, especially those which are heirs to Roman law or socialist revolution, the existence of the state is viewed as the sole means for providing unity, defense, and development. In the latter, reasons of state are often accepted as a right to control information and public opinion, ensuring the general interest in defiance of all private interests. These differing concepts of the state obviously create different interpretations of the right to communicate.[10]

Other fundamental obstacles to democratic communication also exist. Inequalities in the distribution of wealth both domestically and internationally create disparities in information between the rich and the poor. The separation of a culturally advantaged elite from the illiterate masses makes genuinely democratic communication difficult if not impossible. Clearly, an undemocratic political system is a liability to democratic communication, for the right to communicate is often denied along with other basic political rights.

A rigid centralized administrative system may thwart the right to communicate as well. Such a hierarchical system often resists innovation and fails to respond to audience needs. In an overly bureaucratic organization there is seldom adequate public representation in management and policy making; nor is there widespread public access to the means of communication. The same conditions can result from a private system in which control is vested in majority stockholders, the wealthy and powerful, who often exclude the general public. Inadequacy of communication channels, lack of basic infrastructure, and the absence of diversity and choice are also obstacles. So is the exclusion from the communication process of disadvantaged groups such as the poor, handicapped, geographically isolated,

minorities, women, and youth. Lack of knowledge itself
can be an obstacle when people do not have the ability
to understand messages.[11]

These obstacles combine to form a system of vertical communication, the antithesis to democracy in the
communication process. In the vertical system, the flow
of information is usually in one direction, from the top
downward, rather than horizontal, among the communi-
cators and the public. This affects the working style
of communication professionals who consider their job in
terms of "getting the message across," winning and
holding attention by translating information into simple
terms. While these skills are no doubt valuable, they
tend to eclipse public participation. Ordinary people
are often excluded when professional experience and
technological skill are prerequisites to communication.
Improvements in technology usually give additional
skills to the producer and sender of messages.
Unfortunately, they rarely benefit the average citizen
who has a need and a right to communicate.

Jean D'Arcy has summarized vertical communication
as follows:

> Over fifty years' experience of the mass
> media--press, film, radio, television--have
> conditioned us both at the national and
> international levels, to a single kind of
> information flow, which we have come to accept
> as normal and indeed as the only possible
> kind: a vertical, one-way flow from the top
> downwards of non-diversified, anonymous
> messages, produced by a few and addressed to
> all.[12]

Clearly, this is not communication. Rather, it should
be termed "dissemination," a form of one-way message
sending without reciprocity, without exchange. This
produces a large volume of information, but it is
usually offered indiscriminately, not addressed to
distinct, separate audiences and not aimed toward satisfying human needs. In short, vertical communication can
lead to information overload, causing confusion, alienation, passivity.[13]

Today, the vertical flow of information is the
norm, but it is being challenged by groups and
individuals who seek genuinely democratic communication
and demand the right to communicate. An early critic of
the vertical system was the dramatist Berthold Brecht.
In "Radiotheorié," a little known work published in
1932, he wrote:

> The radio must be transformed from a means of
> distribution into a medium of communication.
> Radio might be the most wonderful medium of

> communication for the public, a vast, close-
> meshed network. This it could become if it
> was not only to receive but also to transmit,
> a means given to the listener not only to
> listen but also to speak, a means of putting
> him in touch rather than isolating him. [14]

Contemporary audiences have begun to challenge the
vertical norm as they develop critical attitudes about
what is offered to them. In many countries, citizens'
groups have organized to express concern about media
programming and access. Moreover, the decline in
television viewing time in some countries and opinion
surveys voicing dissatisfaction with media content are
examples of tacit criticism. In advanced countries,
technological innovations such as video tape recorders
and video disk players have changed people's use of the
media, and cable television has made programming more
sensitive to audience needs. These challenges tend to
increase democratic communication as messages become
more diversified, more attuned to specialized needs.
    Other factors have helped to reduce the obstacles
to democratic communication, challenging the vertical
information flow. The right to reply to and challenge
the media as well as increased contact between media
professionals and the public have led to greater access.
The activity of non-professionals in producing and
broadcasting programs, particularly on cable television,
has enabled the public to make use of information
sources and express individual skill and creativity.
Participation in management by representatives of media
users, while usually limited to local media, has brought
the public closer to broadcast organizations and
newspapers. This self-management is a radical form of
participation, permitting a role for the community not
only in programming and news but also in the broader
decision making process. Finally, the development of
alternative channels of communication has fostered
greater democracy. Usually, this involves opposition to
institutionalized, official communication by trade
unions, social groups, dissidents, and minorities. The
alternative channels include traditional methods such as
pamphlets, posters, cartoons, comics, and mimeographed
newspapers as well as more modern means such as super 8
film and video. [15]
    There are many examples of success in the promotion
of democratic communications. The British Broadcasting
Company and Independent Broadcasting Authority have
encouraged the establishment of local radio stations to
meet individual and community needs for access,
self-expression, and participation. When the government
of Italy closed cable television networks and local
radio and television stations set up without
authorization, the constitutional court reversed a

previous decision and excluded these media from the
state monopoly on broadcasting. The United States
Federal Communication Commission decided in 1975 to
increase the number of citizen band radio frequencies
from 23 to 40. The Commission is now studying the
possibility of raising the frequency allocations to 100
in recognition of the citizens' right to communicate
among themselves.[16] In Canada, the provincial government of Saskatchewan made cable television a public
utility. Guidelines require that the company be incorporated on a non-profit basis, provide for user participation in broadcasting as well as management, and permit
community based organizations a role in decision making.
Moreover, the use of satellites provides the inhabitants
of the Canadian far north telephone and television
service, bringing them into the national communication
network for the first time. A number of film workshops
were established by the French to provide local people a
means to make films on neighborhood issues. In the
Federal Republic of Germany, a television station
encourages community groups to make video tapes about
their social concerns and problems, broadcasting them to
stimulate the formation of similar groups in other communities. Yugoslavian information centers produce
newspapers and radio programs about local events and
issues of self-management at the community and regional
level. Radio and television centers publish their
programming proposals so that the public can discuss
them and provide reaction to the proposed programming.
In Australia, 60 ethnic newspapers are published in 20
different languages, maintaining cultural identity and
informing people about events in their country of
origin.[17]

These examples demonstrate that democratic
communication is not simply an ideal. It's an important
value which has been pursued by many states. The right
to communicate is a basic human right, and humane
development will not be achieved without careful attention to democratic communication. Participation, information, and cultural integrity are essential to real
communication, and governments as well as transnational
enterprises must permit individuals and groups to share
in communication if development is to serve humane
needs.

COMMUNICATION FREEDOM

A second communication value which can support
humane development is communication freedom, sometimes
more narrowly termed freedom of the press. Similar to
the ideal of democracy, press freedom is nowhere
absolute. In some countries it is restrained by
government censorship, in others by a lack of financial

resources required to buy time or space in the media. Both situations result in a lessening of communication freedom, constraining the right to communicate and acquire information.

Communication freedom requires the technological means to communicate, but the development of communication means invites control by a government, party, financial or class interest. This control may lead in turn to censorship which ultimately undermines freedom itself. One of the great challenges presented to communication theorists, practitioners, and decision makers is the breaking out of this circular process. No simple formula exists. It makes little sense to demand commercially financed media as a solution to the problem, for in some states, commercial media practice restrictions through the types of messages sent and the limited access permitted. Anyway, this is clearly impractical in many countries. Nor would nationalization of the media solve the problem, for in many state-run media organizations, constraints on freedom are evident.

Various types of states define communication freedom differently. Let's explore these differences by drawing on an analysis of three basic approaches to communication developed by a colleague at the University of Santa Clara, Professor Howard C. Anawalt.[18] The first is a western approach which appears in two forms. The American point of view emphasizes communication freedom as a lively political process and an important commercial activity. This theory arose out of a liberal revolution against the crown and is best represented by the first amendment to the United States Constitution: "Congress shall make no law ... abridging freedom ... of the press."

The basic goal is that individuals and groups should have the maximum possible degree of freedom to send and receive information. Censorship by government is almost absolutely condemned. Freedom of communication is valued as a means to exchange ideas and examine competing political programs. The freedom to express criticism of government and public officials is guaranteed in theory and carried out to a large degree in practice.

Under this theory as espoused by the United States, individuals have a right to prosper economically from their communication. As the economy of the United States grew rapidly, its communication resources have become entwined in commercial activity itself. This has evolved into a system which operates to the advantage of a wide variety of actors including communication based corporations, television and radio networks, newspapers, magazines, publishing houses, individual journalists, and commercial advertisers. The ideals of this theory are partially shared in many western countries. It appears, however, that only the United States has emphasized the right to profit through commercial advertising as a protected freedom.

The western approach also appears in a different form, a Western European viewpoint which posits that communication is not protected from government interference if messages threaten public order. This theory arose in European societies which experienced the decline of feudalism and monarchy, replaced by some form of representative democracy. A good example of this is the Tenth Article of the original French Declaration of the Rights of Man and of the Citizen. It provided that no one could be put under governmental restraint because of his/her opinions so long as the manifestation of those opinions did not interfere with "order established by the law." Great Britain, France, Germany, Italy, and the Scandinavian countries, among others, follow this approach, but most of these nations appear to limit the degree to which the demands of public order actually interfere with freedom of expression. As a result, the European and American viewpoints tend to merge into what is termed the western approach.

A second theory is the developmental journalism viewpoint which emphasizes that communication is an essential process in the establishment of national identity, economic and social strength. The less developed countries have relatively weak economies, and communication is seen as a means to support economic growth and enhance independence and national culture. The process of communication itself, particularly western media imports, seem to be responsible for the creation of a culture alien to many Third World states. Any society which values its own identity wants to assure that indigenous culture is strongly expressed in the media which predominate within its borders.

The less developed countries seek to achieve a position of economic and cultural equality with the rest of the world. States can never be factually equal in power, of course, but they do possess a psychological feeling that equality should be pursued. As a result, they seek to enhance all the elements which make up national identity, encouraging pride and a positive self-image. They also want to increase their power to direct media and communication resources, thereby serving their own people more effectively.

The third theory of communication, the Soviet view, insists that there is no need for a separate freedom of communication beyond the freedom of the Communist Party to speak as the voice of the people, or at least to supervise the messages that flow among the people. This view grew out of the Bolshevik Revolution of 1917 and appears consistent with party organization as conceived by V.I. Lenin and practiced in the Soviet Russian experience. If the party is acting as the vanguard of the masses, then the function of communication is properly executed when the party speaks, for similar to other activities, the party is speaking on behalf of the people.

The Soviet theory of communication is rooted in Marxist economics. According to Marx, all things of value whether they are manufactured goods, food, or even information are composed of contributions from nature and from labor. When individuals and groups exchange goods and services either as barter or with money, a new, more abstract value is attached to the object, its exchange value, which is produced by labor.[19] Marx made his study of capitalism during the nineteenth century's Industrial Revolution. It was evident that the total effort of people living in a capitalist society produced more than the bare minimum for survival. Nevertheless, widespread poverty existed in Germany where Marx was born and in England where he lived and wrote. How could such a state of affairs--poverty in a society of surplus--come about? Marx and his colleague Friedrich Engels argued that the reason was capitalist appropriation of the extra value or surplus value produced by the workers themselves.[20]

Lenin and the Bolsheviks built their revolutionary movement on the concepts of Marx. Their essential task was to liberate surplus value from the capitalist class and put this value back into the hands of those who produced it. All processes in Soviet society, including communication, are based on this primary task, returning control over the means of production to workers. Lenin wrote:

> We must convert--and we shall convert--the press from an organ for purveying sensations, from a mere apparatus for communicating political news, from an organ of struggle against bourgeois lying--into an instrument for the economic re-education of the masses, into an instrument for telling the masses how to organize work in a new way.[21]

In short, Soviet communication must serve the working class and help progress toward a classless society. To do this, there should be less discussion about the intrigues of politicians and more discussion about basic questions of production. The political process is thus secondary to the economic process. This is an accurate, though abbreviated, description of the current Soviet approach to communication. However, it is not fully consistent with the ideal of socialist communication freedom promised by Lenin at the time of the revolution. This inconsistency will be later explored.

Each of these approaches profess, in differing degrees, the ideals of communication freedom. None have completely achieved the ideal, for all restrict communication freedom in some way. To understand how each

approach limits the freedom to communicate and, more
importantly, to suggest a solution to the problem of
control inviting censorship, it is first necessary to
describe the censorship process.

Professor Anawalt notes that in its narrowest
usage, the term "censor" refers to an officer or agency
of the government who has power to restrict the content
of publications or utterances, usually prior to their
distribution. Censorship became an issue of great
importance in seventeenth- century England. By that
time, the British crown had developed an effective
system of control over the circulation of writing. To
publish anything in the realm, it was necessary first to
submit the writing to a government monopoly, the
Stationers' Company, and obtain a license before
publication. This system produced strong intellectual
criticism. John Milton observed that the censor's work
must be boring, for he/she is "made the perpetual reader
of unchosen books and pamphlets, ofttimes huge volumes."
Milton readily admitted that the power of the state must
loom large in his life, but he argued, "the state shall
be my governors, but not my critics; they may be
mistaken in the choice of a licenser as easily as this
licenser may be mistaken in an author ..." The
licensing system was cowardly to Milton for it denied
the strength of truth. "... Who knows not that Truth is
strong next to the Almighty," he wrote. "She needs no
policies, nor strategems, nor licensings to make her
victorious--those are the shifts and defenses that error
uses against her power. Give her but room, and do not
bind her when she sleeps, for then she speaks not true
... ."

The term "censorship" is also used in a broader
sense to refer to a wide range of practices that
interfere with communication freedom. For example, the
International Commission for the Study of Communication
Problems defines it to include prior approval of
writings, post publication restrictions, confiscation of
books, government directives concerning content, boycott
of an author, indexing of prohibited publication, and
the expulsion of individuals from writers and journalists' professional associations. In addition, the commission cites limited access to news sources by
restricting journalists' movements, prohibiting officials to contact journalists, and withdrawal of accre-
ditation or expulsion from the country as severely
limiting communication.

All limits to communication freedom are not
established by public authorities, however. Private
monopolies or concentration of media ownership in
conglomerates often result in a single source of news or
various sources with the same general orientation.
Moreover, advertisers can pose threats to free communication by forcing self-censorship on the media. In
order to maintain the mass audiences necessary to

attract advertising, the media often must dilute news content, appealing to the lowest common denominator of public taste.[24] In addition, the sale of time or space in the media for political messages can limit the ability of less well· financed organizations to make their point. This may not be censorship in its most narrow usage, but it does restrict communication freedom in many countries.

The result of these various restrictions is to direct the course of debate in society. It may be done for good purposes or bad, and there is no doubt that some such directive measures exist in all countries. The extent to which such mechanisms predominate, however, indicates degrees in which society's communication freedom is limited.

The reader familiar with the western approach to communication will wonder how nations committed to this viewpoint can find areas of consensus with countries pursuing Lenin's principle of control over· the media by the Communist Party. In fact, the three approaches to communication described in this chapter each contain at least two professed principles. One is the importance of communication as the foundation of a peaceful and progressive social order. A just and good society will not emerge without some form of social choice and organization, and these choices may require some control over the flow of communication to protect the public order.[25] The other fundamental which is present in the three views of communication is the professed principle that individuals and groups should be able to circulate ideas and proposals (at least economic ones in the Soviet case) with minimum government interference in order that the public may choose among the ideas. Let's explore how the approaches can better live up to their professed principles.

Soviet practice places emphasis on communication controlled by the party in order to achieve public order. However, the Bolsheviks foresaw a time after the revolution when Soviet communication freedom would emerge. They urged that all public groups of sufficient size (approximately 10,000 people) should have access to a fair share of newsprint and other necessary items for communication.[26] The first Bolshevik Decree on the Press made this intention clear, declaring:

> As soon as the new order is consolidated, every administrative measure of restriction with regard to the press will be lifted; it will be granted a full freedom within the limits of its responsibility before the courts, in conformity with the broadest and most progressive press laws.[27]

During the Russian Civil War, Lenin restricted the press severely. Counter-revolutionaries supported by French, British, Japanese, and American troops were pitted against the Bolsheviks, and Lenin denied press freedom to the enemy. "All over the world," he wrote:

> wherever there are capitalists, freedom of the press means freedom to <u>buy up</u> newspapers, to <u>buy</u> writers, to <u>bribe</u>, buy and fake "public opinion" for the <u>benefit of the bourgeoisie</u>. ...

> Can anyone deny that the bourgeoisie in this country has been defeated <u>but not destroyed</u>? That it <u>has gone into hiding</u>? Nobody can deny it.

> Freedom of the press is the R.S.F.S.R., which is surrounded by the bourgeoisie enemies of the whole world, means freedom of political organizations for the bourgeoisie and its most loyal servants ...

> The bourgeoisie (all over the world) is still very much stronger than we are. To place in its hands yet <u>another</u> weapon like freedom of political organizations (= freedom of the press, for the press is the core and founda-tion of political organization) means facili-tating the enemy's task, means helping the class enemy.

> We have no wish to commit suicide, and there-fore we will not do this.[28]

Given Bolshevik military weakness and the allied intervention in the civil war, this approach was not unreasonable at that time.

The Soviet state is no longer in mortal danger, however. One can justifiably question whether continued censorship six decades after the revolution and civil war is still necessary. At the very least, it seems reasonable to suggest that the USSR follow Lenin's views in allowing greater communication freedom in economic matters. Not only would this encourage increased freedom, it would also provide needed information on how to manage the vast and unwieldy Soviet economy. Some progress has already been noted. While censorship is still dominant in the USSR, there was a tendency under Khrushchev to favor greater freedom from administrative control, and it appears that the power of the censors diminished after the death of Stalin.[29] Brezhnev reimposed tighter restrictions, and Andropov is now in the process of establishing his own approach. Wouldn't a relaxation of censorship serve the working class and help bring about the classless society envisioned by Marx and Lenin?

While Soviet practice emphasizes public order and requires greater freedom, Western practice focuses on freedom sometimes to the detriment of better public order. Western thinkers see the press as a means of establishing "a market place of ideas." A free exchange of messages, it is argued, will permit popular choice and the establishment of a society and a government which reflect public will. This approach rests on a social justification, a means of achieving a social good.

Despite its claims of communication freedom, however, the United States falls short of reaching that end. American censorship is not political in nature, but economic inequality results in a kind of restricted communication detrimental to the emergence of a just and good society. Some examples will illustrate the problem. There are basically no governmental restrictions on the United States press. Most newspapers generally attempt to be fair in their political coverage, although some are blatantly one-sided. For example, one Manchester, New Hampshire newspaper makes no apology for supporting conservative candidates, even denying news coverage to liberals whose views it condemns. Even when a newspaper seeks fairness in its news coverage, however, it cannot counter the effect of money on political campaigns. Some candidates with a personal fortune or wealthy supporters can buy political advertisements in newspapers which the opponents cannot afford.

The electronic media, radio and television, can be even more restrictive. The Federal Communication Commission requires that political candidates receive fair coverage by the electronic media. When broadcasters provide free time to one candidate, they must also give free time to the others. When radio or television sells time to one, they must also offer to sell equal time to the others. However, some candidates cannot match the advertising budget of their opponents, and their communication freedom is thereby limited.

Political advertising campaigns have become an important part of American elections. Complex issues are compressed into an expensive 30 second television spot where candidates appear at construction sites or ride on horseback across the plains rather than speak intelligently about their views on public policy. In the New York television market, for example, 30 seconds costs about $12,000. In Washington, D.C., it's $7,500, in Memphis, Tennessee, $1,200 and in Des Moines, Iowa, $1,000. These figures involve only television time. The expense of producing a commercial and media consultant fees are additional.[30]

Political advertising requires candidates to raise

huge sums of money to run for office, making them rely
on political action committees (PACs) formed by trade
associations, corporations, and labor unions. There are
3,700 of these contributors who spent more than $83
million during the 1982 United States congressional
campaign. Approximately 85 percent of this money went
to incumbent members of Congress, reducing the ability
of new candidates to challenge them. One Senator, Orrin
Hatch of Utah, got more than $750,000 from PACs. The
National Association of Realtors' PAC contributed three
million dollars to congressional candidates alone.
While the best financed candidates do not always win,
they do have an unfair advantage based on money. The
political consequences of such financial considerations
can be devastating, a sharp break on political
aspirations.

Money is also used to affect the outcome of initiatives and referendums. In the November 1982 California
election, for example, a number of propositions were
presented to the electorate. Proposition 11 dealt with
a proposal to require a $.05 deposit on beverage con-
tainers to promote recycling and control litter. One
group, "Californians for Sensible Laws," opposed the
proposition, raising $4.1 million to influence the
public through the media. Most of this money came not
from Californians but from large corporations based
outside the state. $775,000 was donated by the Glass
Packaging Institute with headquarters in Washington,
D.C. $300,000 came from the Can Manufacturers Institute
also based in Washington. Other large contributors
included Anheuser-Busch (Budweiser) of St. Louis,
Missouri; Coors Brewing Company of Golden, Colorado;
Coca-Cola of Atlanta, Georgia; and 7-Up of Flint,
Michigan, among other beverage companies. In contrast,
"Californians against Waste," a group supporting the
proposition, raised only $580,510 to influence public
opinion--less than the Glass Packaging Institute alone
gave to the opposition. In the same California Election, another proposition asked voters to decide on hand
gun regulation. Opponents of the proposition outspent
supporters by two to one due to the contributions of gun
companies.[31] All these groups were free to use the
media. However, the power of money made some groups
more "free" than others to present their arguments,
restricting in practice genuine communication freedom
and defeating both propositions 11 and 12.

Some preliminary steps have been taken to curtail
the power of financial wealth in the United States.
Limits have been set on the amount any individual or
group can contribute to congressional campaigns, and in
1970, the partial public funding of presidential
elections was introduced. By checking off a box on the
tax form, citizens can donate $1 of their taxes to a
fund for the presidential campaign, thus reducing the

candidates' heavy reliance on financial supporters. The fund does nothing to support the House of Representatives or Senate campaigns, however, nor is there public funding for state, local, or initiative elections in most parts of the United States. So long as money is necessary to obtain communication freedom, economic censorship will be a major factor in American politics. The freedom to buy votes overrides the principle of using communications to establish a just and good society.

The practice of less developed countries falls somewhere between the poles of the west and the Soviets. Few if any developing states reach the degree of press freedom found in the United States. It took the west centuries to develop the independence of the "fourth estate." Many battles were fought in Europe for a free press, but it was possible as early as the eighteenth century for groups of people on opposing political sides to own newspapers and use them independently from direct governmental control. In most less developed countries, however, a non-governmental press means at present a foreign owned press, for only the state has resources available to establish newspapers and organize their distribution. Only the state has the means to finance broadcasting.[32]

Most western observers simply equate developmental journalism practice with development support communication in the Third World which is designed to promote the cause of economic development. While the two often overlap in countries where the media are government owned, there is an important distinction. Developmental journalism requires communication freedom, for it involves "analytical interpretation, subtle investigation, constructive criticism and sincere association with the grass roots rather than the elite."[33] Developmental communication is an ideal of the 1960s when Third World journalists sought to build grass roots organization and establish the type of alternative press which flourished in New York, London, and Paris. Many journalists who first expressed the need for a developmental approach have now rejected it, after seeing how professionalism and objectivity have been distorted in its name. Nevertheless, some developing countries have established a degree of freedom in their communication media. In India, critical developmental journalism re-emerged in 1978 after Indira Ghandhi's Emergency Decree of June 1975 and subsequent censorship. Nigeria is in the process of returning to greater communication freedom after military rule. Mexico's press is able to criticize government policy, and Egyptian media are more free today than they were under Nasser. Newspapers in other parts of the developing world are struggling for greater communication freedom much like the European press did many years ago.[34]

The intent of the developmental approach is to provide communication which assists national development, independence, and cultural integrity. There is clearly a danger that in practice developmental journalism may become so dominated by officially sanctioned views that competing ideas will have little breathing space. Indeed, there is a substantial risk that the result will be a kind of orthodoxy supported by mere propaganda. However, it is erroneous to declare that such a trend stems from the direct linkage of communication with development policies. No nation, including the United States, foregoes inculcating its dominant ideology through the means at its disposal. In the United States, these means have included a vast public education system and mass media which subscribe to the values of commercialism and the mixed economy. In the Soviet Union, orthodoxy is promoted by the party. For the Third World, information is disseminated through the government and non-government communication systems which comprise a developing society. In short, western orthodoxy is commercial, Soviet orthodoxy is political, and Third World orthodoxy is developmental. To accuse the developmental approach of creating a climate hostile to communication freedom simply because it supports the concept of information as an aid to development is to ignore a fundamental fact--development must occur in the Third World and there is no question that information technology and communication are part of that process. To insist that communication policy be in any way divorced from development in the Third World is like insisting that the sun should not rise in the morning.

There is still reason for concern that developmental journalism practice may be readily turned into propaganda in support of authoritarian regimes. Whenever the government has substantial control over the flow of information, such a result is a real risk. However, the distinction must be made between some Third World leaders who demand that journalists and citizens take their news from the state and those who genuinely believe that some governmental controls are necessary at a certain stage to aid development. There is hope that the latter can tolerate increased communication freedom, allowing their societies humane development. The former doom their countries to authoritarianism where humane values can never be achieved.

Each of these approaches in some way limits communication freedom, for complete freedom is not fully compatible with the requirement of public order. No value is absolute, however. All values have opposites which create tension, and a balance must be struck between freedom and public order. A country may prefer the goal of public order and insist that the communication freedom must not undermine that order. This is the Soviet approach which views order as more valuable than freedom and currently practices censorship even over the exchange of economic information. Alternatively, a nation may simply ignore the need to create a just and good society through communication, condemning government use of the media to achieve social goals. This seems to be the American position. Freedom to communicate is thereby assured, but economic resources are prerequisites to exercising such freedom. Professor Anawalt calls one preferred balance to these extremes the principle of minimum censorship. When coupled with maximum public access, this affirms the values of communication freedom, public order and democracy. This is a clear value judgment, assuming that it is best for individuals and groups to exchange information without the interference of censors. Damage to the public order by communication alone is rare, and restrictions on communication should be kept to a minimum.

How can the minimum censorship/maximum access principle be realized? The answer will vary from one nation to another depending on the organization of political and economic activity. The common ground must be that no country urges censorship in itself as an appropriate goal of government nor prevents citizens from media access because they lack financial resources. The Soviets will no doubt continue much censorship into the foreseeable future. However, once the revolution has been successfully accomplished, as it has, some retreat from censorship at least over the exchange of economic information is in order. The office of the censor is not an appealing one from any viewpoint. Surely if the state is to wither away as Marx had envisioned, the censor must wither away along with it. The western states posit that censorship is a definite evil, yet allow economic resources to stand as an obstacle to communication freedom. Greater public access is essential if all citizens are to experience the freedom to communicate. Less developed countries must acquire information technology for their citizens to communicate, then aim at the broadest possible freedom within the confines of their own need for public order. This balance is possible only if Third World leaders genuinely commit themselves to humane development as a central element to their concept of public order.

Potential consensus on minimum censorship/maximum access among these three approaches to communication is fragile and perhaps illusionary. However, Americans speak earnestly about the free flow of ideas, and Soviets have some basis for concluding that a limited commitment to this goal is not incompatible with their overall objectives. In the Third World, to the extent that each nation escapes from the domination of an authoritarian ruling elite, there is likely to be genuine surge in favor of communication freedom as a value of humane development.

JOURNALIST RESPONSIBILITY

A third communication value necessary for humane development is journalist responsibility. This flows directly from the values of communication freedom and democracy which require certain rights for correspondents who report the news. Journalists must be guaranteed the right to protection. The public's ability to seek and receive information, to participate in the direction of events shaping their lives, and to express themselves freely in an informed way depends on the provision of adequate security for those who gather and disseminate information. The journalist is often an embarrassing witness to sinister events, therefore a target to those who seek to conceal their part in them. This occurs in war, both civil and international, as well as in the reporting of public assemblies and demonstrations opposed by authorities. Extreme forms of pressure include imprisonment, beating, even assassination.

In 1979, for example, an American television correspondent covering the civil war in Nicaragua was deliberately killed by government soldiers, his murder captured on film. Journalists were harassed in Iran during the occupation of the United States Embassy because of their reporting. Eight correspondents simply disappeared in Kampuchea during the Pol Pot regime. These are not isolated incidents. Rather, they are part of a widespread pattern of intimidation. Amnesty International reports that 104 correspondents were jailed or murdered in 25 countries during 1977. In a 15 month period between 1976 and 1978, the International Press Institute claims that 24 journalists were murdered, 57 wounded, tortured, or kidnapped and that 13 newspaper offices were bombed.[35] The public cannot be adequately informed about world events so long as journalists are subjected to such treatment.

There are widely expressed reservations about the desirability of special protection for journalists, however. This could result in their guidance and surveillance by authorities, thwarting their freedom and their ability to gather news independently. Moreover, special protection would probably be made contingent on correspondents' licensing, permitting authorities to decide who is a journalist and prevent those who are not officially approved from working. The best guarantee for the protection of journalists is the extension of human rights for all citizens. Until that occurs, journalism in many countries will be a dangerous occupation, and the public often will be deprived of accurate, reliable information.

A second right flows from the values of freedom and democracy--the right of access, to seek information without hindrance and transmit it safely. Denial of access impoverishes both journalists and the public, restricting the citizens' communication freedom and their need to be informed, a democratic value. Both values of democracy and freedom depend on the right of journalists to practice their craft with integrity and independence.

With rights, independence, and freedom, however, comes responsibility, an essential element of any profession. Just as physicians must be responsible to their patients, teachers to their students, journalists have certain responsibilities as well. With society depending on them for information, they have a vital mission to perform. Unfortunately, many journalists focus on the right to practice their profession freely without fully recognizing the responsibilities associated with journalism. An example drawn from American press coverage will illustrate.

During its 1980 general conference in Belgrade, UNESCO considered certain topics involving world communication as well as a wide variety of other issues including illiteracy, energy, and food production. Of the many items on UNESCO's agenda, only the communication issue was widely reported in the United States, and that topic was reported with a tenor indicating the UNESCO efforts were aimed at stifling a free press. American coverage of the conference is typified by the leading line of an Associated Press study: "Communists and Third World nations used their majority in UNESCO to pass resolutions aimed at getting more control over international news reporting." This same Associated Press line prompted a headline in the Helena, Montana Independent Record: "UNESCO VOTES TO MUZZLE PRESS."

In 1980, the National News Council instructed its staff to study media coverage of the UNESCO meeting to determine whether the press had acted responsibly in acquainting the American public with activities at the conference. The staff examined 448 news clippings and 206 editorials from newspapers in all parts of the United States. Their study revealed that the substance of the UNESCO meeting was scarcely covered in the surveyed news items:

> Not one story emanating from the six weeks' conference dealt with any of the reports, speakers or resolutions on UNESCO's basic activity in combatting illiteracy, developing alternative energy sources, protecting historic monuments, broadening educational programs for scientists and engineers or sponsoring basic research (on) food production, ocean science and scores of other fields.[36]

The only agenda item which received significant newspaper coverage in the United States was UNESCO's critical investigation into the world communication order.

Regarding editorials on the conference, the report found that without exception they expressed apprehension about UNESCO's attention to policy involving the world wide flow of information. 158 of the editorials were strongly hostile, including 27 which suggested that the United States should withdraw from UNESCO altogether if that organization persisted in moves deemed destructive of press freedom. 23 other editorials were more moderately critical of events at Belgrade and made some effort to explain why less developed countries wanted changes in existing communication relationships.

The report revealed that news coverage reinforced the negative attitude of the editorials. The primary source of distortion was the selection of items reported. Neither the scope nor the comprehensiveness of the world debate about the communication order was revealed to American readers. The National News Council acknowledged that American journalists, editors, and publishers may have sincere and perhaps valid apprehension about action UNESCO could take. However, the American media had allowed their own bias to dominate reporting in a manner which is "inconsistent with the spirit of detachment that is invariably set forth as the touchstone of sound news judgement."[37] This conveyed information which was neither complete nor accurate. It was not responsible journalism.

The responsibilities of journalists have been detailed in codes of professional ethics, existing today in 60 different nations.[38] The codes vary considerably from country to country. Some are formulated and adopted by the journalists themselves on a voluntary basis. Others are imposed by law or a decree of the state. Most codes contain some principles which are accepted universally, but there are often significant differences in other aspects of the codes as well as in their formulation and interpretation. Principles such as truthfulness or objectivity are frequently stated in vague, ambiguous terms, and some states require journalists to act in a way which unduly constrains their freedom. Nevertheless, a survey of various codes of professional ethics reveals a number of elements associated with responsible journalism. They are sometimes contradictory, and they produce differing responses from the various approaches to journalism described above.

The most obvious responsibility is to the newspaper or media organization which employs the journalist. Contractual in nature, it requires the journalist to fulfill certain obligations to an employer. This responsibility is often breached less by the reporters and more by their employers when they give orders which are repugnant to journalists. When a media organization refuses to permit coverage of a story or demands coverage which fits preconceived ideas, journalists are placed in a most difficult position. Either they must conform, thereby violating their responsibility or resign from their work. The Soviet approach to communication frequently prevents reporters from covering certain aspects of a story, such as casualties associated with the war in Afghanistan or even a specific event such as an airplane crash. Some media organizations in less developed countries seek to focus attention on positive aspects of national development. This may be based on good motivation, but requiring journalists to omit reports about corruption or the failure of a development project does great harm both to the integrity of the journalists' profession and to the development process. Such problems are unlikely to be corrected if they go unreported.

In the west, an example of an employer's breach of reporters' responsibility is "check book journalism." A newspaper or broadcast organization may pay a person involved in a sensational event, sometimes crime, for exclusive story rights, keeping the person from other newspapers. A professional journalist may be asked to write this person's account as though it were written by the individual personally. Journalists' associations have condemned this practice, pledging not to cooperate, but such "ghost writing" tasks are still sometimes assigned. In this area, ultimate responsibility rests with the publisher or his financial officer who signs the check.

Journalists also have a responsibility to the individuals and groups about whom they report and from whom they receive information. Most codes of professional ethics include language such as "the obligation to refrain from calumny, unfounded accusation, slander, violation of privacy." Responsible journalists must check their facts carefully. If unsure, they must refrain from publishing doubtful items, particularly when they contain unsubstantiated personal material damaging to the reputation of an individual or group. The three approaches to communication tend to agree on this responsibility. Most states have legal remedies for citizens who are libeled by the media, and most journalists take this obligation very seriously.

Many codes also contain language requiring "respect for professional confidentiality" proscribing journalists from revealing the sources of their information when anonymity is requested by the informant. While this seems to appear in most codes, the authorities in many states make demands on journalists to reveal their sources in violation of this element of responsibility. This is both unjust and unwise. It is unjust to demand

that journalists violate their own codes as a condition
of continued employment, for it undermines the
integrity of their profession and the credibility of
their reports. It is unwise, for sources of information
will quickly disappear unless confidentiality is
assured.

A third kind of responsibility is social in nature,
entailing obligation toward society. In the western
approach, responsibility to society is often viewed in
terms of keeping the public informed, serving as "the
fourth estate" by a critical examination of government.
Readers have a right to be sure that published material
is factual, based on sound investigation and research.
Codes of professional conduct refer to this obligation
when they demand "objectivity, accuracy, truthfulness
and the nonmisrepresentation of facts." While most
western reporters are serious about this aspect of their
work, there have been exceptions. For example, a series
of articles in the Washington Post dealt with a child
heroin addict. The articles were vivid and well written
with major impact. In fact, the series won the reporter
a nomination for a Pulitzer Prize, subsequently with-
drawn when it was discovered that no such child addict
existed. The journalist simply invented the facts,
violating a responsibility to her readers.

Codes of professional ethics also frequently call
for "responsibility to the public and its rights and
interests and in relation to national, racial and
religious communities (and) the nation ..." The Soviet
approach agrees with this element but in practice claims
that the party rather than the journalist determines
what is in the public interest. This makes the reporter
little more than a mouthpiece for authority, denying the
very responsibility which a code of ethics seeks to
achieve. The developmental approach focuses on the need
to write about indigenous culture and development policies. So long as the journalists remain free to investigate, analyze, and criticize, their responsibility to
society is fulfilled. When they are required to write
uncritically about development, however, their responsibility to the public is not discharged.

One aspect of social responsibility is the public's
right of correction and reply. This is recognized in
many countries by law, in others by codes of ethics, and
in still others on a voluntary basis. One must make a
distinction between the two rights, however, and the
responsibilities based on them. For issues involving a
simple difference of opinion, it is usually impractical
to require a reply for all who disagree with an article
or news item. The newspaper or broadcast organization
must consider the degree of public interest, the importance of the issue, and the available time or space. In
contrast, inaccurate facts or untruthful reporting
should always be corrected. In some countries, notably

the United Kingdom and Sweden, the right of reply and correction is governed by codes of conduct often applied with the supervision of press councils. The United States relies on the media themselves to volunteer the public's right of reply and correction. In many other states, the right of correction and reply may be readily available, but only to those citizens approved by the authorities.

Clearly, reporters do not have a social responsibility to intelligence agencies who sometimes seek to infiltrate the journalists' profession and provide agents with a cover for espionage. Journalists' associations have condemned this practice, emphasizing that it is unethical for reporters to perform intelligence services. The associations recognize that this practice reduces the credibility of journalists as a profession and endangers foreign correspondents. However, a code of conduct condemning this is not much help for journalists in a situation where the state controls both the intelligence agency and the media.

Finally, journalists have an international responsibility to the world community, the family of humanity. Most codes of professional conduct devote little, if any, attention to this responsibility, however. They are usually formulated to regulate relations among journalists and individuals, employers, and national society. However, there are some issues which transcend the individual and the nation, affecting all of humankind. For example, questions about war and arms control, hunger and poverty, and violations of human rights are particularly important. They require sensitive and humane reporting, focusing world attention on the dangers of nuclear war, the consequences of national and international inequality, and the systematic abuse of human rights in many countries.

Journalists are particularly suited to foster the emergence of a public vitally concerned with peace and aware of the tragedy of war and the arms race. There is an obvious connection between media and public opinion; and it has been suggested that the media can contribute more to shaping attitudes about violence and war than the traditional socializing agents of the family and the school. In fact, many people in the United States spend more time each day using mass media, particularly television, than pursuing any other activity except sleep and work.[39]

In the past, journalists have sometimes exercised this power responsibly. Television coverage during the last few years of United States' involvement in Vietnam, for example, was an important element in turning the American public against that war and toward demands for a negotiated settlement. In some situations, however, journalists have been used for irresponsible ends. During times of riot or civil strife, for example, journalists and television cameras often unwittingly encourage violence by their very presence. Many spectacular acts of terrorism are planned and executed to be guerilla theater, capturing world attention through the media. Research has suggested that people's fear of crime is associated more strongly with mass media's emphasis on violence than with the actual frequency of violent crime in a community.[40] Journalists have the power to spread fear and to stimulate violent acts, despite intentions. Why shouldn't they exercise their power to free people from distrust and fear to assert their opposition to war, violence, and the arms race?

Journalists have an international responsibility to build a commitment to peace in the minds of men and women, and that responsibility has been specified in many international agreements, resolutions, and instruments. As early as 1930, the League of Nations considered the press's potential contribution toward the building of peace. In 1947, the United Nations General Assembly condemned all forms of propaganda which jeopardize peace.[41] More recently, the international community have reiterated on several occasions that incitement to war and war mongering are condemned by the United Nations Charter.[42]

Article 20 of the International Covenant on Civil and Political Rights, established in 1966 and ratified by many states, declares: "(1) any propaganda for war shall be prohibited by law; (2) any advocacy of national, racial or religious hatred that constitutes incitement to discrimination, hostility or violence shall be prohibited by law."[43]

The United Nations General Assembly's Special Session on Disarmament in 1978 adopted specific resolutions which refer to the media's contribution to the promotion of peace. It declared: "It is essential that not only governments but also the people of the world recognize and understand the dangers of the present situation." To accomplish this, "member states should be encouraged to ensure a better flow of information with regard to the various aspects of disarmament, to avoid dissemination of false and tendentious information concerning armaments and to concentrate on the danger of escalation of the arms race and on the need for general and complete disarmament under effective international control."[44] The 1982 Second Special Session on Disarmament expressed similar concerns and recognized the potential of journalists' contribution to the cause of peace.

Through these instruments, agreements, and resolutions, the international community have called on journalists to further the cause of arms control. Recognizing that journalists have tremendous power through the use of information, these international bodies are requesting them to use their power responsibly by condemning militarism, nuclear war, and the arms race. Such condemnation is beyond the politics of national interest. Rather, it is a step to further the common interest of humanity in peace and the future safety of our planet.

Many journalists embrace these ideas about responsibility to the world community and seek a common code of professional ethics which would incorporate them. Indeed, a number of efforts have been made to draft such a code, some on a regional, others on an international level. The First Pan-American Press Conference meeting in Washington adopted an International Code of Journalistic Ethics as early as 1926, reaffirming it as the creed of the Inter-American Press Association in 1950. The United Nations Sub-Commission on Freedom of Information and the Press prepared a draft International Code of Ethics for Information Personnel over three decades ago. Its provisions called for freedom of information as a basic human right, truthfulness and accuracy, correction of false and harmful news, professional confidentiality, and condemnation of slander or misrepresentation of facts. Concerning international responsibility, the draft included a requirement for journalists reporting about foreign countries to acquire necessary knowledge about those countries and write about them fairly and accurately. In 1954, the General Assembly decided to take no action on the draft. Instead, they forwarded it to professional associations and media organizations for voluntary acceptance.

Other non-governmental international bodies have taken similar action. In 1955, the Inter-American Association of Broadcasters accepted a Declaration of Ethical Principles, and member organizations developed their own codes based on these principles. The International Federation of Journalists adopted a Declaration of Journalists Duties in 1954, and a Declaration of Duties and Rights of Journalists was adopted by 6 journalists' trade unions of the European Community in 1975. The International Organization of Journalists, the Latin American Federation of Journalists, and an organization of Arab journalists have also been concerned with international responsibility.[45]

Developmental journalists are particularly enthusiastic about professional codes which call for responsibility in the reporting of world poverty and the process of development. Soviet journalists emphasize responsibility for the maintenance of peace as well as coverage of the north-south inequality of wealth. The latter seem less willing, however, to accept responsibility for reporting violations of human rights, at least in their own countries. Western journalists are divided on the issue of common codes demanding responsibility. Many Western Europeans accept the idea while most American journalists reject the notion that they have an obligation to promote any cause, no matter how noble. These latter journalists believe their professional values require them to be absolutely neutral. To condemn the arms race, for example, would require taking sides on an issue, and this would interfere with their professional objectivity. They believe that it is the editor's or columnist's job to state opinion, not that of the reporter.[46] Objectivity is their ideal, aimed at but never fully realized.[47] However, one must question how any human being, including a journalist, can be objective about nuclear war and the destruction of life on earth. This does not mean that journalists should report all news subjectively. Nuclear war is of such paramount importance, however, that it should be condemned by all professions, even by the journalists who ordinarily seek to be objective in their reporting. Other vital issues such as human rights and world inequality demand similar subjective involvement and responsibility.

Objections to professional responsibility for the condemnation of war, human rights violations, and world poverty are found among journalists who personally embrace a desire for greater equality, a respect for human rights, and a fear of nuclear war. These reporters feel that the circulation of information is itself a basic human right. The best contribution journalists can make to resolve important international problems, they believe, is to exercise their occupation with complete freedom and objectivity. As a result, reporting should not be influenced by international responsibility for the maintenance of peace, the promotion of human rights, or the lessening of world inequality.

All journalists must seriously consider the relationship among communication values, however. Reporters who do not act responsibly lessen their right to be free. Reporters who are denied freedom cannot be expected to act responsibly. Without the values of free and responsible journalism, democratic communication will not be fully realized. A balance must be struck in which none of these values is jeopardized, for democracy is best served when free journalists report responsibly.

Given fundamental variations among the three approaches to communication, it is clear that such a balance among communication values must be arrived at differently. In the Soviet Union, progress toward economic democracy has not been matched in political democracy, and genuinely democratic communication seems to be a long way off. Nor have Soviet journalists been given much freedom even in the reporting of economic news. Some progress has been made since Stalin's death, particularly in Hungary and Yugoslavia. However, important experiments toward greater freedom and democracy

which occurred in Czechoslovakia and Poland were crushed
by intimidation and force. Soviet style journalists can
never reach a level of professional responsibility so
long as their fundamental freedom of inquiry is so
widely restrained. Greater freedom to communicate must
be established before democracy or responsibility can
flourish.

In the United States, some progress toward
increased responsibility has been achieved on a
voluntary basis. Press councils have been established
to investigate public complaints of distorted, false, or
misleading reporting. Ombudsmen have been appointed by
some newspapers to examine the complaints of readers and
focus attention on the failures of the press to cover
specific news items. Many American newspapers now
include op-ed pages, published opposite the editorial
page, which invite articles by outside writers. Letters
to the editor are published by virtually all American
newspapers, giving citizens the right to express their
opinions on matters of public concern.[48]

Some American papers have also focused greater
attention on questions of international importance. For
example, in August 1982, The San Jose Mercury published
a series of articles on the nuclear arms race by
scholars and government officials from east and west.
The Washington Post and The New York Times have included
feature articles on the need for women's rights. The
Los Angeles Times published a series of articles on
poverty in Mexico, and The Christian Science Monitor has
devoted considerable attention to issues of development
and the north-south gap in wealth. Due to United States
constitutional guarantees against restrictions on the
press, these efforts must be voluntary in nature, and
American journalists could never submit to mandatory
international codes of professional conduct. In the
United States it is the journalists, editors, and publishers themselves who must espouse the value of responsible journalism. Some have done so, but many more must
follow before America's free press will become fully responsible and achieve democratic communication values.

In Western Europe, a number of institutions have
helped establish greater democratic communication and
responsibility. Press councils, first established by
Sweden in 1916, now exist in Austria, the Federal Republic of Germany, the United Kingdom, Denmark, Finland,
and the Netherlands, among other countries. Essentially, these press councils insure that all journalists
respect the principles of ethical conduct which have
been established by their profession. Some include members of the public while others are limited to professional journalists and their employers. The former
are more democratic, for they permit lay persons to
speak for citizens who feel unfairly treated by the
press.

Other such institutions have also emerged. A 1959 Italian law set up Courts of Honor for the press in which the plaintiff is represented by a lawyer while a representative for the defendant is chosen from a list of persons nominated by the council of the Order of Journalists. There is no press council in Belgium, but a Council of Discipline and Arbitration handles citizen complaints. In Sweden and some other Scandinavian countries, a press ombudsman deals with breaches of professional ethics. The Swedish ombudsman handles approximately 400 complaints annually and can initiate action as well. Swedish newspapers must publish the verdict of an investigation when the press is at fault, and the ombudsman can also require newspapers to publish disclaimers or correct erroneous facts. Sweden also has an ombudsman who deals with radio and television, while Finland's Press Council handles complaints regarding broadcasting. So long as these institutions are free from government control, as they are in Western Europe, the values of communication freedom, democracy, and responsibility are promoted.[49]

Communication values are continually evolving in less developed countries. Press freedom is still a new concept in most Third World states where journalists are often treated more like civil servants than independent professionals. These countries are only now acquiring the means to communicate, and authorities are often unwilling to risk losing control. Democracy is difficult, if not impossible, in nations where legitimacy and political order have not emerged; and many governments will not permit freedom of communication in situations where economic growth has been unable to provide political contentment or where social and ethnic cleavages are disruptive. In the Philippines, for example, it is forbidden to criticize the president, his family, or the armed forces. Marcos wants no challenge to his personal rule operating under a kind of martial law. The media in Malaysia cannot discuss the government's language policy, special privileges given to the Malay ethnic group, or the citizenship policy for non-Malays. This is due in part to a long history of communal rioting and ethnic suspicions which have torn that country apart. President Suharto of Indonesia simply shut down the press by state decree during the 1978 election campaign. He wanted no criticism of his national ideology nor any possibility of popular dissent to his electoral plans.[50]

With these restraints on communication freedom and democracy, it is surprising that many reporters in less developed countries have achieved any level of responsibility at all. Despite problems, however, the Third World contains many brave journalists, struggling against authoritarian regimes to inform the public. While they cannot take a "publish and be damned" attitude toward their work, they are often successful in exercising responsibility and some freedom under severe handicaps. Some must write their material in a constrained manner, seeming to examine the social, political, and economic affairs of other countries while really criticizing their own. Others simply refuse to be a party to censorship, giving up their careers rather than compromising their integrity. As the less developed countries gradually build their economies, integrate their societies, and establish less authoritarian political systems, it is hoped that a unique balance among the values of communication democracy, freedom, and responsibility will emerge. Without it, development will not achieve genuinely humane ends.

NOTES

1. MacBride, p. 166.
2. The Universal Declaration of Human Rights adopted by the General Assembly of the United Nations, December 10, 1948, article 19.
3. Jean D'Arcy, "The Right to Communicate," Research paper number 36, The International Commission on the Study of Communication Problems on file at UNESCO headquarters, Paris and the International Institute of Communication, London, reprinted in Crisis in International News: Policies and Prospects, Jim Richstad and Michael H. Anderson, editors (New York: Columbia University Press, 1981), pp. 118-36.
4. Gunnar Naesselund, "UNESCO Conference: 'Balanced Communication'," Intermedia, vol. 2, no. 5 (March 1975), p. 17.
5. Gunter, p. 104. For a discussion on the right to communicate and its component elements, see L.S. Harms and Jim Richstad, Evolving Perspectives on the Right to Communicate (Honolulu, Hawaii: East-West Communication Institute, 1977) and L.S. Harms, Jim Richstad and Kathleen A. Kies, Right to Communicate: Collected Papers (Honolulu, Hawaii: University Press of Hawaii, 1977).
6. "Statement by the participants in the Dag Hammerskjold Third World Journalist Seminar, New York, August 19-September 12, 1975," Development Dialogue, no. 1 (1976), p. 108.
7. Elie Abel, "Communication for an Interdependent, Pluralist World" in Richstad and Anderson, p. 111.
8. Gunter, pp. 105-07; Hidetoshi Kato, "Four Rights of Communication: A Personal Memorandum" in Richstad and Harms, pp. 79-82.
9. Gunter, pp. 102-03.
10. Jean D'Arcy in Richstad and Anderson, pp. 125-26.
11. MacBride, pp. 166-68.
12. Jean D'Arcy in Richstad and Anderson, p. 122.

13. Régis Debray, "Education and the Media," _Libération_, Paris, June 22, 1979.

14. Bertold Brecht, "Radiotheorie," _Gesammelte Werke_ Band VIII (Berlin, 1932), p. 129.

15. MacBride, pp. 168-69.

16. D'Arcy in Richstad and Anderson, p. 130.

17. MacBride, p. 169.

18. The analysis of three basic approaches to communication presented here was developed by Professor Howard C. Anawalt of the University of Santa Clara Law School. The extensive research concerning these viewpoints and the comparisons were done by Professor Anawalt, and the present author has incorporated substantial direct statements from a previously unpublished manuscript by Professor Anawalt in the text on pages 119 through 132. The author also refers the reader to what he considers a somewhat similar typology which appears in Fred S. Siebert, Theodore Peterson, and Wilbur Schramm, _Four Theories of the Press_ (Urbana, Illinois: University of Illinois Press, 1956, 1971).

19. Karl Marx, _Critique of the Gotha Programme_ (New York: International Publishers, 1938), pp. 3-11 and _Capital_, vol. 1 (New York: International Publishers, 1967), pp. 35-48.

20. Friederich Engels, _Socialism: Utopian and Scientific_ (Moscow: Foreign Languages Publishing House, 1958), pp. 91-93.

21. V.I. Lenin, original version of the article "The Immediate Tasks of the Soviet Government, April 28, 1918," _Lenin About the Press_ (Prague: International Organization of Journalists_, 1972), p. 333.

22. This is the usual understanding of the term as used in the west. The origin of the word "censor" seems to be the title of a Roman official who was responsible for drawing up a registry of citizens and supervising public morals. Various officials, especially church leaders exercised such power in the intervening centuries, but the arrival of Gutenburg press linked censorship to the circulation of ideas in print. Today, the electronic media--radio and television--are also often censored. See the _Oxford English Dictionary_ ("censor") and Paul O'Higgins, _Censorship in Britain_ (London: Thomas Nelson and Sons Ltd., 1972), p. 11.

23. John Milton, _Areopagitita_ in Complete Poems and Major Prose_, Merritt Y. Hughes, editor (New York: The Odyssey Press, 1957), pp. 734, 736, 747; reprinted in _Versions of Censorship_, John McCormick and Mairi MacInnes, editors (Garden City, NY: Doubleday & Company, 1962), pp. 8-34 with commentary on pp. xiii-xx, 3-7.

24. MacBride, pp. 139-40.

25. The importance of public order in communication is reflected in article 19 of _The International Convention for the Protection of Civil and Political Rights_ which provides that everyone shall have the right to freedom of expression, but this basic right may be subject to certain specific regulations provided by law and public order (_ordre public_) or of public health and morals. American jurists accept the notion that no one has the freedom to shout "fire" without cause in a crowded theater.

26. "On the Formation of a Commission to Probe the Dependence of Bourgeois Newspapers on Banks, Draft Resolution, November 17, 1917," Lenin About the Press, p. 208.

27. V.I. Lenin, "Supplement Decree on the Press," November 10, 1917, Lenin About the Press, pp. 205-06.

28. V.I. Lenin, Letter to G.I. Myasnikov, August 5, 1921, Lenin About the Press, p. 199.

29. Mark W. Hopkins, Mass Media in the Soviet Union (New York: Pegasus, 1970), pp. 123-29.

30. These figures based on December 1982 telephone interviews.

31. These figures are based on reports filed with California Secretary of State, March Fong Eu as reported in The San Jose Mercury, October 22, 1982 and a New York Times article on the Federal Election Commission report of April 28, 1983.

32. Smith, pp. 148-52.

33. Shelton A. Gunarante, "Media Subservience and Developmental Journalism," Communications and Development Review, vol. 2, no. 2 (Summer, 1978), pp. 3-7.

34. Smith, p. 150.

35. MacBride, p. 235 and Jim Richstad, "Transnational News Agencies: Issues and Policies" in Richstad and Anderson, p. 251.

36. A.H. Raskin, "US News Coverage of the Belgrade UNESCO Conference," Journal of Communication, vol. 31, no. 4 (Autumn 1981), p. 164.

37. Raskin, p. 173.

38. The discussion of codes of ethics is based on MacBride, pp. 241-49; "Extracts from Deontological Codes of Journalists," Research paper number 20 submitted to the International Commission on the Study of Communication Problems on file at UNESCO headquarters, Paris and the International Institute of Communication, London; and Clement J. Jones, Mass Media Codes of Ethics and Councils (Paris: UNESCO, 1980). These codes are taken from some 60 countries.

39. Television and Behavior: Ten Years of Scientific Progress and Implications for the Eighties, vol. I, pp. 3, 36-44. Also see George Comstock, Steven Chaffee, Nathan Katzman, Maxwell McCombs and Donald Roberts, Television and Human Behavior (New York: Columbia University Press, 1978). The A.C. Nielson Company, a television audience research organization estimates that daily television viewing in the average American home was six hours, 44 minutes in 1982.

40. Walter B. Jaehnig, David H. Weaver and Frederick Fico, "Reporting Crime and Fearing Crime in Three Communities," Journal of Communication, vol. 31, no. 1 (Winter 1981), pp. 88-96. These researchers suggest that the role of many journalists is "to shock, shame and titilate rather than to inform." Also see George Gerbner et al, "Cultural Indicators: Violence Profile no. 9," Journal of Communication, vol. 28, no. 3 (Summer 1978), pp. 176-207 and "The Demonstration of Power: Violence Profile no. 10," Journal of Communication, vol. 29, no. 3 (Summer 1979), pp. 176-96. In his October 21, 1981 testimony before the Subcommittee on Energy and Commerce, United States House of

144

Representatives, Gerbner stated that television teaches the lessons of violence and power.

41. "Measures to be taken against Propaganda and the Inciters of a New War," United Nations General Assembly Resolution 110 (II), November 3, 1947 and "False or Distorted Reports," United Nations General Assembly Resolution 127 (II), November 5, 1947.

42. This is based on The Charter of the United Nations and Statute of the International Court of Justice, Preamble, Chapter I, Article 1, Sections 1 and 2; and Article 2, Sections 3 and 4.

43. International Covenant on Civil and Political Rights, adopted and opened for signature, ratification and accession by United Nations General Assembly Resolution 2200A (XXI), December 16, 1966, part III, article 20.

44. United Nations General Assembly First Special Session on Disarmament, "Final Document" S-10/2, June 30, 1978, Article II, Section 15 and Article III, Section 105.

45. MacBride, pp. 243-44.

46. See Keith Fuller, "AP: Covering the World" in Richstad and Anderson, pp. 271-74.

47. George Gerbner, "Ideological Perspectives and Political Tendencies in News Reporting," Journalism Quarterly, vol. 41 (summer 1964), pp. 495-508.

48. Abel in Richstad and Anderson, pp. 113-14.

49. MacBride, pp. 245-48.

50. Smith, pp. 154-55.

Conclusion: Requirements
for Humane Development

> The philosophers have only interpreted the
> world in various ways. The point, however, is
> to change it.
>
> Karl Marx

This book has examined the potential of information
technology and communication for supporting humane
development in Third World countries. IT, the means of
communication coupled with the values of democracy,
freedom, and responsibility can assist in social integration, individual awareness, popular participation,
mass mobilization, economic growth, and the redistribution of wealth and power. IT can increase the ability
of governments to meet basic needs, resulting in greater
public support for the institutions of the state and the
increased cohesion of the nation. With careful technological choice and adaption leading eventually to indigenous research and development, Third World countries
can achieve greater independence and self-reliance. The
possibilities for information technology's support of
development are many. What will it take to make the
potential a reality?

Many Third World leaders have focused their
attention on the creation of a new world communication
order, condemning the current order for its imbalance in
information flows, the dominance of Third World cultures
by the west, and the technological dependency it seems
to perpetuate. The developing nations' desire for a new
communication order is part of their demand for a new
economic order which, it is hoped, would reduce the gap
between the wealth of the north and the poverty of the
south. Both new orders demand a global approach to the
problems of development founded on more equity of
rights, greater equality, and increased participation.
Both call for the termination of Third World dependency
in economics and communication alike which produce
greater inequality and a waste of natural, material, and

human resources. The logical connection between the two orders is information, a special kind of basic resource performing important social functions. In one sense, information technology and communication are a prerequisite for a new economic order because communication is the basis for all economic activity among individuals, groups, and nations.

A new world communication order as described by many Third World spokespersons is not a likely prospect, however.[1] The interests and power of wealthy countries and corporations are simply too great to permit a radical restructuring of global communication. Even if a new order were established immediately, the less developed countries would require additional measures to realize the potential of information technology and communication. Action must be taken on individual, national, regional, and non-governmental as well as international levels if the Third World is to benefit fully from information technology. Let's conclude by examining some necessary steps at each of these levels.

INDIVIDUAL LEADERSHIP

No amount of information technology will lead to humane development unless individual leaders in less developed countries are genuinely committed to progressive change. These individuals must have power to lead, charisma to inspire, and empathy to feel the misery and suffering of their country's poor. They must be willing to share some of their power, recognizing that humane development will not occur without popular participation in government and a redistribution of society's resources among the poor.

These are rare qualities, to be sure, and few leaders in advanced or developing states possess the desire or the ability to put national interest ahead of personal aggrandizement. The situation is not completely hopeless, however, for there are examples of such leadership. Gandhi, Roosevelt, MacBride, Bolivar, Nyerere, Allende and Hammarskjöld have placed concern for people ahead of personal interest, accomplishing much. Other leaders have the potential for greatness, and they will have to realize that potential if Third World countries are to experience humane development.

There will be obvious resistance to sharing wealth and power from strong forces both domestic and international. Entrenched elites whose privilege would be threatened by development as well as certain multinational economic interests will oppose redistribution. Leaders must be powerful enough to overcome such resistance and caring enough to use their power to benefit the poor. Charisma would be an important asset in mobilizing the poor to support development and organizing them to counter resistance from privileged elites. The struggle will be bitter and prolonged, of course, its outcome by no means assured. However, a country cannot develop if the majority of its citizens remain powerless and poor. The masses must demand progressive change, and greater equality will have to be supported by strong, benevolent leaders.

Third World leaders must also recognize limitations in restructuring the world order, concentrating on a more pragmatic approach which mutes the strident rhetoric of the past. They should avoid politicized hyperbole, taking a reasoned look at reality.[2] Western states are not moved by empty threats, charges of malice, or mutual recriminations. They may be induced to cooperate in achieving limited goals by reasonable arguments based on factural analysis and coincidental interests. Without such cooperation, it will be difficult to achieve even the more simple changes necessary for a more just and equitable world communication order.

In short, realizing the potential of information technology and communication to support development assumes wise, benevolent, responsible leadership. Where this is present, IT can be an important development tool. In its absence, IT could be used to thwart freedom and democracy, keeping the poor in misery and bondage. Humane development and the fulfillment of basic needs would therefore remain an unachievable goal, useful for rhetorical pronouncements but impossible to attain in reality.

NATIONAL PLANNING

Wise, benevolent leadership is not enough, however, to achieve development through information technology. Third World countries must engage in comprehensive planning with communication part of an overall development plan rather than an incidental service left to chance.[3] The object is to use the unique capacities of all types of communication from traditional to modern, making people aware of their rights, bringing unity out of diversity, and motivating individuals as well as communities.

Providing information to support projects in agriculture, nutrition, health, family planning, and industry should be part of the development plan, and this will require adequate financing. Clearly, communication for the rural poor must be subsidized by the state, a difficult task for many less developed countries. However, sources of revenue do exist. For example, a Third World country could tax commercial advertising as well as establish differential communication pricing which requires greater expenditures by the more prosperous, urban elite. The development plan must set a high priority on revenue for communication if other programs are to be successful.

Additionally, the national development plan should encourage two-way communication. Ahmadou Mahtar M'Bow, Director-General of UNESCO, made this clear in a July 1981 speech to a meeting of Third World information ministers in the Cameroon:

> You cannot ask for the creation of conditions which will redress the current imbalance in the field of communication without looking at the state of information in your own countries. You cannot legitimately ask for a free and balanced flow of information at the international level while denying this at a national level.[4]

Obviously, decision makers need to transmit information about development projects downward to the entire society. Equally important is the need for horizontal communication among diverse social and cultural groups and upward communication to express aspirations and needs. The public must also participate in evaluating the social implications of new information technology including its consequence for culture, employment, life styles, and relevance to the needs of the poor. In this way, communication can be integrated into overall development to establish and support national goals.

Within the framework of a development plan, each state will need to establish a set of priorities for the essential elements of its communication system involving print media, broadcasting, and telecommunications as well as related training and production facilities. In rural areas or small towns where a sufficient level of literacy exists, community newspapers could inform people and encourage greater literacy. Book production in all a country's languages might also be encouraged with an adequate distribution system for books, periodicals, and newspapers.

Clearly, the establishment of community based radio stations within a comprehensive national radio network capable of reaching remote rural areas should be preferred to television, which is more costly and often relies more heavily on foreign programming. Within the network, local radio stations should be encouraged to address community needs. Where television already exists or will be introduced, a national capability for producing broadcast material is required to overcome excessive dependence on imported programs. The use of low cost, small format video systems and other appropriate technology would encourage the production of material relevant to community development efforts, provide diversified cultural expression, and stimulate public participation in the media.

For person-to-person communication, an information technology infrastructure could extend postal services and telecommunications networks to rural areas through the use of small electronic exchanges and point-to-point satellite technology. Such an infrastructure would help provide the rural poor with more information from a variety of sources and permit increased communication among themselves and with the decision makers.

Less developed countries must also plan to establish centers for the collection of technical information from inside the country and abroad. They should obtain the essential equipment necessary for basic data processing and facilities for computer analysis of data obtained from remote earth microwave sensing. They should give greater attention to informatics, establishing centers to assess technological alternatives, centralize purchases and encourage domestic production of software. For many states, this will require regional cooperation as part of the development plan.

The role of communication in education and culture must also be considered as part of the development plan. A major policy objective for less developed countries is the elimination of illiteracy and the provision of free elementary education for all. To these ends, communication can supplement formal schooling with non-formal education through radio, television, and correspondence. Programmed instruction by "schools of the air" could assist in this effort with community listening or viewing groups organized to utilize a limited number of receivers and provide peer support for educational activities.

National communication policies must foster cultural identity and creativity while encouraging knowledge of other cultures. Indigenous artists, musicians, and film makers as well as local theater and dance companies should have access to mass media. In multicultural countries, all ethnic and linguistic groups need to be included in radio and television broadcasting. Moreover, Third World states must establish guidelines on advertising content and the values it promotes. These guidelines should be consistent with efforts to preserve cultural identity, with particular attention devoted to the impact of advertising on children and adolescents. The public could react against inappropriate advertising through complaint boards or consumer review committees.

Finally, on the national level, countries must adopt measures to expand their sources of information. Secrecy provisions and other constraints to a free flow of information should be reduced. Censorship and arbitrary control over communication should be eliminated. Where certain restrictions are considered necessary, these should be based on law, subject to judicial review, and consistent with principles established by the United Nations Charter, The Universal Declaration of Human Rights, and other international agreements. Correspondents, both domestic and foreign, should have free access to information sources covering the full spectrum of opinion within a country, and they should be able to transmit the information unhindered. It is only through a genuinely free flow of information that decision makers can learn about the success or failure of their own development projects and about innovative programs elsewhere. National and regional news agencies can facilitate this process.

While providing journalists with the freedom to communicate, Third World countries have the right to demand responsibility and accountability. Governments should not be involved in this, however. Press councils, the media ombudsman, and citizen action through complaint boards are probably the best way to encourage greater accountability within the framework of a free press, and journalists themselves must adopt codes of conduct setting responsible guidelines.

These suggestions--the integration of communication into the overall development plan, setting priorities, concern about culture and education, and the expansion of information sources--may be accomplished at the national level. Even leaders who are serious about humane development may find some of the suggestions difficult as they are tempted to exercise strict control over newly acquired information technology. Without a free, two-way flow of information, careful planning, and citizen participation, however, humane development will remain an illusion.

REGIONAL ASSOCIATION

A third set of requirements necessary to realize the potential of information technology and communication involves regional association. Technological research and development, production, training, and finance may be accomplished more effectively by pooling the resources and talents of less developed countries. This is especially important for the poorer and smaller Third World states, but regional cooperation can benefit even the more affluent less developed countries as well.

Autonomous research and development programs are not feasible for all developing countries in every area of technology. Consequently, a regional approach to research and development with various states specializing in different aspects of technology is necessary. These efforts should be linked to specific projects aimed at satisfying basic human needs as defined by the regional states in association with each other.

Cooperative efforts would also help less developed countries choose and adapt technology more effectively, avoid the acquisition of obsolete or overly sophisticated technology, and obtain required spare parts and components. Moreover, a larger regional market in technology might encourage advanced states and corporations to give greater attention to appropriate technology, for the larger market could make this a profitable enterprise.

Regional data banks and information processing centers should also be established to avoid excessive dependence on the advanced industrialized states. This could encourage less developed countries to produce their own software, gain management experience, and set up the kinds of data bases necessary to promote development. It would also lead to greater cooperation in the evaluation of new information technology and management techniques, making the monitoring of development projects more efficient.

A regional approach can lead to greater professional sharing as well, establishing networks of institutions and individuals working in communication and the exchange of valuable experience. This could result in the formation of cooperative education and training facilities to provide managers, technicians, and maintenance personnel for media and production organizations. Moreover, such joint activities promote the sharing of films, radio and television programs about common concerns produced by the less developed countries themselves.

Cooperative regional associations already exist in news activities. For example, the Caribbean Area News Agency (CANA) brings together the English speaking nations of the Caribbean in a common endeavor. The Middle East News Agency (MENA) represents cooperative efforts among Arab States. Small, isolated islands in the South Pacific region are linked by satellite to share news and other information. On a broader level, the Nonaligned News Agency Pool provides centers for the collection and distribution of reports sent to the pool by more than 40 participating national news agencies. Despite its meager resources, the pool symbolizes important cooperative activities for less developed countries.[5]

Finally, regional economic and financial cooperation must be encouraged. A group of states may find it easier to raise capital for communication projects on a multilateral rather than a bilateral basis. Exchanging information on trade negotiations, relationships with banks and multinational enterprises would strengthen countries in a region, and cooperation in economic forecasting would promote more accurate planning. Regional measures can be an important supplement to the national approach in making information technology and communication an effective development tool.

INTERNATIONAL COOPERATION

Leadership, national planning and regional association involve action by the less developed countries themselves. Cooperation with the advanced states is also important to achieve the full benefits of information technology and communication for development. This requires action by international organizations as well as bilateral agreements. Two important areas for cooperative efforts are technology and access.

Historically, international support for information technology has been marginal at best, and many development projects have not achieved success due to a lack of communication resources. In the future, international assistance for information technology and communication must be given a high priority as a basic component of efforts in other areas such as health, agriculture, industry, and education. This assistance must be compatible with the less developed countries development plans, and it should be designed to support broad programs rather than individual projects.

Advanced countries must also agree to a greater exchange of relevant technical data, practicing their principles of a free flow of information in technology as well as in news and entertainment. To reduce inequality, it is necessary to establish cooperative networks for the collection, retrieval, and processing of technical information regardless of institutional or geographical frontiers. The Universal System for Information in Science and Technology (UNISIST) program of UNESCO is an existing framework for this cooperation, currently providing fully operational networks such as the Agricultural Science and Technology Information System and the International Nuclear Information System. This program and others like it in the United Nations organization should further expand their activities.

Cooperation at the international level should also aim at a systematic identification of existing data processing infrastructures in specialized areas as well as greater participation in the planning, programs, and adminstration of these data infrastructures by less developed countries. A thorough analysis of commercial and technical measures necessary to improve the use of informatics by Third World states is required. Moreover, agreement on priorities for research and development on informatics beneficial to less developed countries would encourage the world's scientists to use their talent in helping the poor.

The Third World needs greater access to international communication as well, and this cannot be achieved without international agreement. For example,

air postal rates affect the flow of newspapers, periodicals, and books among developing states and between
advanced and less developed countries. Currently, the
Universal Postal Union permits its members to offer a 50
percent optional discount for mailing printed matter,
but more drastic cuts are needed to increase the flow of
information and stimulate the production of publications
in less developed countries. The Universal Postal Union
is strongly influenced by the Ministries of Post and
Telegraph of its member states, most from the Third
World, who consistently lose money on their operations.
As a result, they may resist any large scale reductions
in rates which would further cut their revenue. The
primary aim of such ministries is not revenue, however.
They are instruments of development for information and
culture, and their policies should be consistent with
larger, national goals.[6]

Telecommunications tariffs are another area where
practice has limited the access of developing countries.
The current tariff structure of Intelsat is the result
of numerous agreements at national and international
levels, and it is in serious need of reform. Less
developed countries pay a higher price for satellite
telecommunications transmission. It costs less for
Intelsat to provide service to large users, the advanced
states, than to start and stop repeatedly the smaller
transmissions sent by less developed countries.[7] However, news and other kinds of transmissions vital for
development projects should get preferential treatment.
Intelsat needs to recognize that the social benefits of
international communication should override considerations about revenue maximization. Industrial states
could pay marginally higher tariffs for telecommunications to help Third World countries in an area important
to their development. Developing states must also
attempt to negotiate preferential tariffs on a regional
or group basis.

Use of the electro-magnetic spectrum and the geosynchronous orbit has also tended to limit the access of
less developed countries. These finite, supranational
resources are the common heritage of humankind, however,
and the first come, first served basis for their allocation as practiced in the past is a disadvantage for
Third World countries. They rejected this approach at
the 1979 World Administrative Radio Conference in Geneva, favoring instead the reservation of these resources
for their future use. Over the next few years, a series
of conferences will be held to set new allocation policies, and less developed countries should press for
their fair share of these resources, possibly on a
regional basis. They may be unable to use certain bands
of the spectrum and the geosynchronous orbit at the
present time, but they could lease their allocation to
advanced states until Third World countries are ready to

use them.

Finally, it would be useful for the United Nations to be equipped with a more effective information system including access to satellite communication and international broadcasting capability. This would permit the United Nations to monitor world events more closely and transmit messages about development, peace, and human rights to all people.

NON-GOVERNMENTAL ACTION

Issues of communication and information technology transcend the nation state and the international system, requiring action by non-governmental bodies such as transnational enterprises and journalists' associations. Corporations, news agencies and journalists exercise considerable power in communication beyond the control of states or international organizations. Their concern, good will, and responsibility could do much to assist less developed countries in the use of information technology.

No one expects transnational corporations to engage in enterprises purely out of altruism. These companies must respond to the interests of their stockholders and return a profit on their investment. Nevertheless, some transnationals have recognized a social responsibility to countries in which they do business, understanding that a less impoverished Third World could, in the long run, mean more business and more profit. With a larger market for small scale information technology made possible by regional cooperation, the transnational companies may find it profitable to do research and development on technology more appropriate to the needs of less developed countries. Third World states should encourage this, declining the more complex and expensive equipment produced for advanced countries. Moreover, authorities in developing countries should demand information about the transnationals' activities to understand more fully the working of the world economy. They should also require the transnationals to comply with specific conditions defined by national legislation and development plans. The likelihood of compliance would be enhanced if these requirements were based on regional cooperation.

One group of transnationals plays a particularly important role in international communication. The four major news agencies have dominated global news reporting and, as we have seen, they have not always covered the Third World with thoroughness and sensitivity. This has caused resentment in less developed countries, but it has also been detrimental to the advanced states' understanding of the Third World.

To overcome this problem, traditional criteria for

news selection and reporting--news values--need to be reassessed if audiences throughout the world are to obtain a more comprehensive picture of events and proc- esses in developing countries. Ethnocentric thinking distorts the perceptions of all human beings, including journalists, despite their attempts at objectivity. The very act of selecting some facts for publication while rejecting others can lead to incomplete understanding and distortion. The wire services must recognize this, devote more attention to news about the Third World, and supplement it with background reports to put news into perspective.

This is no small task for the transnational news agencies. Their power in world news may be great, but their resources are severely limited. In 1978, for example, one large agency operated on revenues of $112 million.[8] For comparison, IBM, one of the largest transnational corporations, generated annual sales of $18 billion in the same year, and the University of Hawaii, located in a state with a population of one million, spends around 50 percent more each year than the entire Associated Press world and domestic service.[9]

Despite their limited resources, the wire services are making some changes in coverage of the Third World. The overwhelming proportion of news about the advanced states seems to have lessened somewhat, and more news about the less developed countries is gradually appear- ing in western media.[10] Moreover, the flow of news among the developing countries has increased, although this may be the result of the Nonaligned News Agency Pool rather than the wire services.[11] The transnation- al news agencies have moved slightly away from exclu- sive, conventional "event journalism" toward "process journalism," seriously asking what constitutes news.[12] News agency editors have cautioned their correspondents to avoid gratuitous remarks which could be considered slurs and to balance their reporting of development failures with coverage of successes. Many are seriously trying "to see things from the viewpoint of the society they are covering."[13] Finally, the western news agen- cies have entered into a number of cooperative arrange- ments with national news agencies in less developed countries. This can provide a better understanding of Third World news needs as well as share experience and expertise.

In short, western journalists are trying to raise their standards, seeking to attain greater professional- ism and responsibility. This would be facilitated by requiring broader educational preparation for journal- ists in specific fields such as economics, technology, political science, or sociology. Clearly, reporters who are given foreign assignments should have language training as well as an understanding of the history, politics, economics, and cultures of the countries they cover.

These standards cannot be imposed, however. Nor should they depend solely on the good will of individual journalists employed by media institutions and managed by editors who can help or hinder professional responsibility. Voluntary associations of journalists are the best way to establish ethical principles and higher professional standards of responsibility. The journalists and their editors must decide themselves to provide more sensitive and thorough coverage to the process of development.

Given requirements involving wise, benevolent leadership, national planning, regional, international and non-governmental cooperation, it may seem that humane development is impossible despite the wonders of information technology. There is obviously reason for pessimism. It is certain that Third World countries will use IT and communication to support development, however. The issue is not whether this will occur. Rather, it is a question about what kind of development information technology will foster.

Two broad, future scenarios are possible.[14] In one group of developing countries, informatics and mass media may be used to oppress through authoritarian controls, surveillance, and propaganda. The police state or military junta will find information technology invaluable to keep their people enslaved, realizing the dehumanization and totalitarian manipulation expressed in George Orwell's Nineteen Eighty-Four:

> Behind Winston's back the voice from the telescreen was still babbling away about pig-iron and the overfulfillment of the Ninth Three-Year Plan. The telescreen received and transmitted simultaneously. Any sound that Winston made, above the level of a very low whisper would be picked up by it; moreover, ... he could be seen as well as heard. There was of course no way of knowing whether you were being watched at any given moment. How often, or on what system, the Thought Police plugged in on an individual wire was guesswork. It was even conceivable that they watched everybody all the time. But at any rate they could plug in your wire whenever they wanted to. You had to live--did live, from habit that became instinct--in the assumption that every sound you made was overheard, ... every movement scrutinized.[15]

In another group of states, information technology may lead to increased freedom, democracy, and human dignity, bringing closer together masses and elite, public and leaders, advanced and Third World countries

in a common effort at human liberation. IT could result
in a celebration of life, expressed by the Jesuit
philosopher Teilhard de Chardin:

> The last blank spaces have vanished from
> the map of mankind. There is contact every-
> where, and how close it has become! Today,
> embedded in the economic and psychic network
> ... two great human blocks alone remain con-
> fronting one another. Is it not inevitable
> that in one way or another these two will
> eventually coalesce? Preceded by a tremor, a
> wave of 'shared impulse' extending to the very
> depths of the social and ethnic masses in the
> need and claim to participate, without dis-
> tinction of class or colour, in the onward
> march of human affairs, the final act is
> already visibly preparing ... Who can say
> whether, coiled back upon our own organism,
> our combined knowledge of the atom, of hor-
> mones, of the cell and the laws of heredity
> will take us? Who can say what forces may be
> released, what radiations, what new arrange-
> ments never hitherto attempted by Nature, what
> formidable powers we may henceforth be able to
> use, for the first time in the history of the
> world? This is Life setting out upon a second
> adventure from the springboard it established
> when it created humankind.[16]

Unfortunately, the latter group of countries will
most probably constitute a small minority. Perhaps few
societies, developing or advanced, really care about the
poor. Those which do will find information technology
and communication an important means to change the
world, breaking the chains of poverty and achieving a
more noble human existence.

NOTES

1. Spokespersons for a fundamental revision of the World
Communication Order include Mustapha Masmoudi, "The New World
Information Order," Journal of Communication, vol. 29, no. 2
(Spring 1979), pp. 172-79; Tapio Varis, "World Information
Order," Instant Research on Peace and Violence, vol. 4 (1976),
pp. 143-47; Juan Somavia, "International Communication and Third
World Participation," Development Dialogue, no. 2 (1977), pp.
138-44 and The Transnational Power Structure and International
Information (Mexico City: ILET, 1978) passim; and Kaarle
Nordenstreng, "Behind the Semantics--A Strategic Design," Journal

of Communication, vol. 29, no. 2 (Spring 1979), pp. 195-98.

2. Mort Rosenblum suggests this in "Reporting from the Third World," pp. 834-35.

3. Many of these recommendations are based on MacBride, Part V, pp. 253-72; additionally, some of the suggestions are presented in "Toward an American Agenda for a New World Order of Communications," a conference report of the United States Commission for UNESCO (Washington, D.C.: Department of State, 1980), Roger Tatarian, Rapporteur.

4. Interview with Ahmadou Mahtar M'Bow, Director General of UNESCO in _South_, no. 13 (November 1981), pp. 10-11.

5. Michael H. Anderson, "Emerging Patterns of Global News Cooperation" in Richstad and Anderson, pp. 335-36, 338-39.

6. Abel in Richstad and Anderson, pp. 106-07.

7. _Ibid._

8. This figure comes from "News Media Offered UPI Partnerships," _New York Times_, September 23, 1979.

9. Jim Richstad, "Transnational News Agencies: Issues and Policies" in Richstad and Anderson, p. 249.

10. Robert L. Stevenson, "Beyond Belgrade: Prospects for a Balanced Flow of Information," a paper presented to the International Studies Association Annual Meeting, Philadelphia, Pa., March 1981.

11. David H. Weaver, G. Cleveland Wilhoit, Robert L. Stevenson, Donald L. Shaw and Richard R. Cole, "The News of the World in Four Major Wire Services," a paper for inclusion in the final report of the "Foreign Images" project of the International Association for Mass Communication Research, UNESCO, 1980; Wilbur Schramm, "International News Wires and Third World News in Asia" in Richstad and Anderson, pp. 198-220; and Richstad in Richstad and Anderson, pp. 246-47.

12. Anderson in Richstad and Anderson, pp. 326-27; also see William J. Stover and Howard C. Anawalt, "Who Makes News: An Inquiry into the Creation and Control of International Communication," _Peace Research_, vol. 15, no. 1 (January 1983, pp. 15-23 and no. 2 (June 1983), pp. 36-41.

13. Mort Rosenblum, _Coups and Earthquakes: Reporting the World for America_ (New York: Harper and Row, 1979), p. 13.

14. A.A.L. Reid, "New Telecommunications Services and their Social Implications" in _Telecommunications in the 1980's and After_, James Lighthill, editor (Cambridge, England: Cambridge University Press, 1978), pp. 181-82.

15. George Orwell, _Nineteen Eighty-four_ (New York: Harcourt, Brace, and Company, 1949), p. 4.

16. Pierre Teilhard de Chardin, _The Future of Man_ (New York: Harper & Row, 1964), pp. 175-77.

Bibliography

Abel, Elie, "Communication for an Independent World," in Crisis in International News, Jim Richstad and Michael Anderson, editors. New York: Columbia University Press, 1981, pp. 98-116.

Adelman, I., and Morris, C.T. Economic Growth and Social Equity in Developing Countries. Stanford Cal.: Stanford University Press, 1973.

Aggarwala, Narinder K., "News with Third World Perspectives: A Practical Suggestion," in The Third World and Press Freedom, Phillip C. Horton, editor. New York: Praeger, 1978.

Allen, Irving Lewis, "Social Integration as an Ongoing Principle," in Mass Media Policies in Changing Cultures, George Gerbner, editor. New York: John Wiley and Sons, 1977, pp. 235-50.

Amin, Samir. Accumulation on a World Scale. New York: Monthly Review Press, 1974.

Amin, Samir. Unequal Development. New York: Monthly Review Press, 1975.

Anderson, Michael H., "Emerging Patterns of Global News Cooperation," in Crisis in International News, Jim Richstad and Michael H. Anderson, editors. New York: Columbia University Press, 1981, pp. 318-43.

"Asia's Special Need for Satellite Links," Intermedia, vol. 9, no. 4 (July 1981), pp. 86-88.

Baran, Paul A. The Political Economy of Growth. New York: Monthly Review Press, 1957, 1962.

Bargnouri, S.M., "The Role of Communication in Jordan's Rural Development," Journalism Quarterly, vol. 51 (Autumn 1974), pp. 418-24.

Bennett, J.M., and Kalman, R.E., editors. Computers in Developing Nations. Amsterdam: North Holland Publishing Company, 1981.

Block, Clifford; Foote, Dennis R.; and Mayo, John K., "SITE Unseen: Implications for Programming and Policy," Journal of Communication, vol. 29, no. 4 (Autumn 1979), pp. 114-24.

Boon, Gerald, "Some Thoughts on Changing Comparative Advantage," Institute of Development Studies Bulletin, vol. 13, no. 2 (March 1982), pp. 14-18.

Brecht, Bertold, "Radiotheorié," Gesammelte Werke, Band VIII. Berlin: 1932.

159

160

Bryson, Lyman, editor. The Communication of Ideas. New York: Harper, 1948.

Casey-Stahmer, Anna, "The Era of Experimental Satellites: Where Do We Go From Here?" Journal of Communication, vol. 29, no. 4 (Autumn 1979), pp. 137-44.

Charter of the United Nations and Statute of the International Court of Justice.

Chen, P., and Miller, A.E., "Lessons from the Chinese Experience: China's Planned Birth Program and its Transferability," Studies in Family Planning, vol. 6, no. 10 (1975), pp. 354-66.

Chenery, H.; Ahluwalia, M.S.; Bell, C.L.G.; Dulog, J.H.; and Jolly, R. Redistribution with Growth. London: Oxford University Press, 1974.

Cole, J.P. The Development Gap. New York: John Wiley and Sons, 1981.

Communication Policy in Brazil. New York: UNESCO, 1975.

Comparative Advantage in an Automated World, Institute of Development Studies Bulletin, vol. 13, no. 2 (March 1982).

Comstock, George; Chaffee, Steven; Katzman, Nathan; McCombs, Maxwell; and Roberts, Donald. Television and Human Behavior. New York: Columbia University Press, 1978.

"Conceptual and Policy Framework for Appropriate Industrial Technology." Vienna, Austria: United Nations Industrial Development Organization, ID/232/1, 1979.

Cooper, Kent. Barriers Down. New York: J.J. Little and Ives Company, 1942.

D'Arcy, Jean, "The Right to Communicate," International Commission for the Study of Communication Problems, Research paper number 36 on file at UNESCO Headquarters, Paris and the International Institute of Communication, London.

Debray, Régis, "Education and the Media," Libération, June 22, 1979.

Deutsch, Karl W. Nationalism and Social Communication, Cambridge, Mass.: M.I.T. Press, 1966.

Dorman, William A., and Omeed, Ehsan, "Reporting Iran the Shah's Way," Columbia Journalism Review (January/February 1979), pp. 27-33.

The Economist, October 17, 1981.

Editor and Publisher, The Fourth Estate, vol. 112, no. 1, January 6, 1979.

Edquist, Charles, and Edquist, Ole, "Social Carriers of Science and Technology," Discussion paper 123. Lund, Sweden: Lund University Research Policy Program, October 1978.

Employment, Growth, and Basic Needs. Geneva, Switzerland: International Labor Organization, 1976.

Enahoro, Peter, "Building a New Africa," interview in World Press (August 1982), pp. 24-27.

Engels, Friedrich. Socialism: Utopian and Scientific. Moscow: Foreign Languages Publishing House, 1958.

Foster-Carter, Aiden, "From Rostow to Gunder Frank: Conflicting Paradigms in the Analysis of Underdevelopment," World Development, vol. 4, no. 3 (March 1976), pp. 167-80.

Frank, André Gunder, "The Development of Underdevelopment," <u>Monthly Review</u>, vol. 18, no. 4 (September 1966), pp. 17-31.

Frank, André Gunder. <u>Latin America: Underdevelopment or Revolution</u>. New York: Monthly Review Press, 1969.

Freidel, Frank. <u>Franklin D. Roosevelt Launching the New Deal</u>. Boston: Little, Brown, and Company, 1974.

Freire, Paulo. <u>Pedagogy of the Oppressed</u>. New York: Herder & Herder, 1970.

Fuglesang, Andreas. <u>Applied Communications in Developing Countries: Ideas and Observations</u>. Motala, Sweden: Borgström tryckeri AB, 1973.

Fuller, Keith, "AP: Covering the World," in <u>Crisis in International News</u>, Jim Richstad and Michael H. Anderson, editors. New York: Columbia University Press, 1981, pp. 271-73.

Fyson, Nancy Lui, editor. <u>The Development Puzzle</u>. London: Center for World Development Education, 1979.

Gerbner, George, <u>et al</u>., "Cultural Indicators: Violence Profile No. 9," <u>Journal of Communication</u>, vol. 28, no. 3 (Summer 1978), pp. 176-207.

Gerbner, George, <u>et al</u>., "The Demonstration of Power: <u>Violence Profile No. 10</u>," Journal of Communication, vol. 29, no. 3 (Summer 1979), pp. 176-96.

Gerbner, George, "Ideological Perspectives and Political Tendencies in News Reporting," <u>Journalism Quarterly</u>, vol. 41 (Summer 1964), pp. 495-508.

Gerbner, George, editor. <u>Mass Media Policies in Changing Cultures</u>. New York: John Wiley and Sons, 1977.

Gerbner, George, and Gross, Larry, "Living with Television: The Violence Profile," <u>Journal of Communication</u>, vol. 26, no. 2 (Spring 1976), pp. 172-99.

Goulet, Dennis. <u>The Uncertain Promise: Value Conflicts in Technology Transfer</u>. New York: IDOC/North America, 1977.

Griffin, Keith, and Khan, Azizur Rahman, "Poverty in the Third World: Ugly Facts and Fancy Models," <u>World Development</u>, vol. 6, no. 3 (March 1978), pp. 295-304.

Grunig, J.E., "Communication and the Economic Decision Making of Columbian Peasants," <u>Economic Development and Cultural Change</u>, vol. 18 (1971), pp. 580-97.

Gunaraute, Shelton A., "Media Subservience and Developmental Journalism," <u>Communications and Development Review</u>, vol. 2, no. 2 (Summer 1978), pp. 3-7.

Gunter, Jonathan F. <u>The United States and the Debate on the World "Information Order"</u>. Washington, D.C.: Academy for Educational Development, Inc., 1979.

Hall, B.L. <u>Developmental Campaigns in Rural Tanzania</u>. Cambridge, England: International Council for Adult Education, 1975.

Hamelink, Cees. <u>The Corporate Village</u>. Rome: IDOC Europe Dossier Four, 1977.

Harms, L.S., and Richstad, Jim, editors. <u>Evolving Perspectives on the Right to Communicate</u>. Honolulu, Hawaii: East-West Communication Institute, 1977.

162

Harms, L.S.; Richstad, Jim; and Kie, Kathleen A., editors. <u>Right to Communicate: Collected Papers</u>. Honolulu, Hawaii: University Press of Hawaii, 1977.

Harrison, Paul. <u>The Third World Tomorrow</u>. New York: Penguin Books, 1980.

Hirschman, A.O., "Changing Tolerance for Inequality in Development," <u>Quarterly Journal of Economics</u>, vol. 57, no. 4 (November, 1973), pp. 544-62.

Hopkins, Mark W. <u>Mass Media in the Soviet Union</u>. New York: Pegasus, 1970.

Horton, Philip C., editor. <u>The Third World and Press Freedom</u>. New York: Praeger, 1978.

Howkins, John, "The Management of the Spectrum," <u>Intermedia</u>, vol. 7, no. 5 (September 1979), pp. 10-22.

Howkins, John, "The Next Wave of Television," <u>Intermedia</u>, vol. 9, no. 4 (July 1981), pp. 14-26.

Howkins, John, "What is the World Administrative Radio Conference?" <u>Journal of Communication</u>, vol. 29, no. 1 (Winter 1979), pp. 144-49.

Hudson, Heather E., "Implications for Development Communication," <u>Journal of Communication</u>, vol. 29, no. 1 (Winter 1979), pp. 179-86.

Hughes, Merritt Y., editor. <u>John Milton: Complete Poems and Major Prose</u>. New York: The Odyssey Press, 1957.

Huntington, Samuel P. <u>Political Order in Changing Societies</u>. New Haven, Conn.: Yale University Press, 1968.

"Industry 2000, New Perspectives." New Delhi, India; United Nations Industrial Development Organization, ID/237, August, 1979.

<u>Information Resources Policy Annual Report</u>, vol. 2. Cambridge, Mass.: Harvard University Project on Information and Resources, 1976.

Inkeles, Alex, and Smith, D.H. <u>Becoming Modern: Individual Change in Six Developing Countries</u>. Cambridge, Mass.: Harvard University Press, 1963.

International Commission for the Study of Communication Problems, "A Glimpse into Communication Statistics," Research paper number 6 on file at UNESCO Headquarters, Paris and the International Institute of Communication, London.

International Commission for the Study of Communication Problems, "Communications: What do We Know?," Research paper number 9 on file at UNESCO Headquarters, Paris and the International Institute of Communication, London.

International Commission for the Study of Communication Problems, "Extracts from Deontological Codes of Journalists," Research paper number 20 on file at UNESCO Headquarters, Paris and the International Institute of Communication, London.

"International Cooperation with a View to the Use of Computers and Computational Techniques for Development," United Nations Economic and Social Council Resolution E/RES/1571(L), May 1971.

Islam, Nurul, "Economic Interdependence Between Rich and Poor Nations," Third World Quarterly, vol. 3, no. 2 (April 1981), pp. 230-50.

Jaehnig, Walter B.; Weaver, David H.; and Fico, Fredrick, "Reporting Crime and Fearing Crime in Three Communities," Journal of Communication, vol. 31, no. 1 (Winter 1981), pp. 88-96.

Janowitz, Morris. The Community Press in an Urban Setting. New York: The Free Press, 1952.

Jones, Clement J. Mass Media Codes of Ethics and Councils. Paris: UNESCO, 1980.

Joshi, G.V., "India's Eye in the Sky," South, no. 14 (December 1981), p. 39.

Kaplinsky, Raphael, "The Time Bomb in Computers," The Guardian, May 21, 1982.

Kato, Hidetoshi, "Four Rights of Communication: A Personal Memorandum" in Evolving Perspectives on the Right to Communicate, Jim Richstad and L.S. Harms, editors. Honolulu, Hawaii: East-West Communication Institute, 1977, pp. 79-82.

Katz, Elihu, "Can Authentic Cultures Survive New Media?," Journal of Communication, vol. 27, no. 2 (Spring 1977), pp. 113-21.

Kennan, George F. Democracy and the Student Left. Boston: Little, Brown, and Company, 1968.

Kincaid, D.L., et al. Mothers' Clubs and Family Planning in Rural Korea. Honolulu, Hawaii: East-West Communication Institute, 1973.

Lazarfeld, Paul, and Merton, Robert, "Mass Communication, Popular Taste, and Organized Social Action," in The Communication of Ideas, Lyman Bryson, editor. New York: Harper, 1948, pp. 95-118.

Lenin, V.I., "The Immediate Tasks of the Soviet Government, April 28, 1918," Lenin About the Press. Prague: International Organization of Journalists, 1972, pp. 336-37.

Lenin, V.I., "Letter to G.I. Myasnikov, August 5, 1921," Lenin About the Press, Prague: International Organization of Journalists, 1972, pp. 198-201.

Lenin, V.I., "On the Formation of a Commission to Probe the Dependence of Bourgeois Newspapers on Banas, Draft Resolution, November 17, 1917," Lenin About the Press. Prague: International Organization of Journalists, 1972, p. 208.

Lenin, V.I., "Supplement Decree on the Press," November 10, 1917, Lenin About the Press. Prague: International Organization of Journalists, 1972, pp. 205-06.

Lerner, Daniel. The Passing of Traditional Society. Glencoe, Ill.: The Free Press, 1958.

Lighthill, James, editor. Telecommunications in the 1980's and After. Cambridge, England: Cambridge University Press, 1978.

Liu, Alan P.L. Communes and National Integration in Communist China. Berkeley, Cal.: University of California Press, 1971.

MacBride, Sean, et al. Many Voices, One World. New York: UNESCO, 1980.

164

Martin, James. Future Developments in Telecommunications, second edition. Englewood Cliffs, N.J.: Prentice-Hall, 1977.

Marx, Karl. Capital, volume I. New York: International Publishers, 1967.

Marx, Karl. Critique of the Gotha Program. New York: International Publishers, 1938.

Masmoudi, Mustapha, "The New World Information Order," Journal of Communication, vol. 29, no. 2 (Spring 1977), pp. 172-79.

M'Bow, Ahmadou Mahtar. Interview in South, no. 13 (November 1981), pp. 10-11.

McAnany, Emile G., editor. Communication in the Rural Third World. New York: Praeger, 1980.

McCormick, John, and MacInnes, Mairi, editors. Versions of Censorship. Garden City, N.Y.: Doubleday and Company, 1962.

McNelly, John R., "International News From Latin America," Journal of Communication, vol. 29, no. 2 (Spring 1979), pp. 156-63.

Milton, John, Areopagitita, in John Milton: Complete Poems and Major Prose, Merritt Y. Hughes, editor. New York: The Odyssey Press, 1957, pp. 716-49.

Mody, Bella, "Programming for SITE," Journal of Communication, vol. 29, no. 4 (Autumn 1979), pp. 90-98.

Naesselund, Gunnar, "UNESCO Conference: 'Balanced Communication,'" Intermedia, vol. 2, no. 5 (March 1975), pp. 16-18.

Nag, B., "Appropriate Computerization--An Instrument of Development and Social Change in Developing Countries" in Computers in Developing Nations, J.M. Bennett and R.E. Kalman, editors. Amsterdam: North Holland Publishing Company, 1981, pp. 53-57.

The New York Times, September 23, 25, 28, 29, November 10, 17, 22, 24, 25, December 4, 1979, and April 28, 1983.

Nordenstreng, Kaarle, "Behind the Semantics--A Strategic Design," Journal of Communication, vol. 29, no. 2 (Spring 1979), pp. 195-98.

O'Higgins, Paul. Censorship in Britain. London: Thomas Nelson and Sons Ltd., 1972.

"On the Formulation of a Commission to Probe the Dependence of Bourgeois Newspapers on Banks," Draft Resolution, November 12, 1917, Lenin About the Press. Prague: International Organization of Journalists, 1972, p. 208.

Orwell, George. Nineteen Eighty-Four. New York: Harcourt, Brace, and Company, 1949.

Parker, Yakup, "Informatics and Development: UNESCO's Approach for the 1980's," in Computers in Developing Nations, J.M. Bennett and R.E. Kalman, editors. Amsterdam: North Holland Publishing Company, 1981, pp. 11-20.

Pipes, G. Russel, "National Policies, International Debates," Journal of Communication, vol. 29, no. 3 (Summer 1979), pp. 114-23.

Porat, M.U., "Global Implications of the Information Society," Journal of Communication, vol. 28, no. 1 (Winter 1978), pp. 70-80.

Pye, Lucien. Communication and Development. Princeton, N.J.: Princeton University Press, 1963.

Raskin, A.H., "US News Coverage of the Belgrade UNESCO Conference," Journal of Communication, vol. 31, no. 4 (Autumn 1981), pp. 164-74.

Rateau, Oliver, "Informatics: Evolution and Use in the 1980's, with Particular Reference to Developing Countries," in Computers in Developing Nations, J.M. Bennett and R.E. Kalman, editors. Amsterdam: North Holland Publishing Company, 1981, pp. 3-9.

Reid, A.A.L., "New Telecommunications Services and Their Social Implications," in Telecommunications in the 1980's and After, James Lighthill, editor. Cambridge, England: Cambridge University Press, 1978, pp. 175-84.

Rice, Ronald E., and Parker, Edwin B., "Telecommunication Alternatives for Developing Countries," Journal of Communication, vol. 29, no. 4 (Autumn 1979), pp. 125-36.

Richstad, Jim, and Anderson, Michael H., editors. Crisis in International News. New York: Columbia University Press, 1981.

Richstad, Jim, "Transnational New Agencies: Issues and Policies," in Crisis in International News, Jim Richstad and Michael H. Anderson, editors. New York: Columbia University Press, 1981, pp. 98-116.

Righter, Rosemary, "Who Won?," Journal of Communication, vol. 29, no. 2 (Spring 1979), p. 192-94.

Robinson, Glenn O., "Regulating International Airwaves: The 1979 WARC," Virginia Journal of International Law, vol. 21, no. 1 (Fall 1980), pp. 1-54.

Rogers, Everett M., editor. Communication and Development. London: Sage, 1976.

Rogers, Everett M., "Communication and Development: The Passing of the Dominant Paradigm," in Communication and Development, Everett M. Rogers, editor. London: Sage, 1976, pp. 121-48.

Rogers, Everett M., "New Perspectives on Communication and Development: An Overview," in Communication and Development, Everett M. Rogers, editor. London: Sage, 1976, pp. 7-14.

Rogers, Everett M., "The Rise and Fall of the Dominant Paradigm," Journal of Communication, vol. 28, no. 1 (Winter 1978), pp. 64-69.

Rosenblum, Mort. Coups and Earthquakes: Reporting the World for America. New York: Harper and Row, 1979.

Rosenblum, Mort, "Reporting from the Third World," Foreign Affairs, vol. 55, no. 4 (July 1977), pp. 815-35.

Rostow, Walt W. The Economics of Take-Off into Self-Sustaining Growth. London: Macmillan for the International Economic Association, 1963.

Rostow, Walt W. Politics and the Stages of Growth. Cambridge, England: Cambridge University Press, 1971.

Rostow, Walt W. The Process of Economic Growth. London: Oxford University Press, 1953, 1960.

Rostow, Walt W. The Stages of Economic Growth: A Non-Communist Manifesto. Cambridge, England: Cambridge University Press, 1960, 1971.

Sagasti, Francisco R., "Knowledge is Power," Mazingira, no. 8 (1979), pp. 28-33.

San Jose Mercury, October 22, 1982.

Sarder, Ziauddin, "Separate Development for Science," Nature, vol. 273 (May 18, 1978), pp. 176-77.

Schramm, Wilbur, "International News Wires and Third World News in Asia," in Crisis in International News, Jim Richstad and Michael H. Anderson, editors. New York: Columbia University Press, 1981, pp. 198-220.

Schramm, Wilbur. Mass Media and National Development. Stanford, Cal.: Stanford University Press, 1964.

Shore, Larry, "Mass Media for Development," in Communication in the Rural Third World, Emile G. McAnany, editor, New York: Praeger, 1980, pp. 19-45.

Shukla, Sneklata, "The Impact of SITE on Primary School Children," Journal of Communication, vol. 29, no. 4 (Autumn 1979), pp. 99-103.

Siebert, Fred S.; Peterson, Theodore; and Schramm, Wilbur. Four Theories of the Press. Urbana, Ill.: University of Illinois Press, 1956, 1971.

Singer, Hans. Technologies for Basic Needs. Geneva: International Labor Organization, 1977.

Singham, A.W. The Non-Aligned Movement in World Politics: A Symposium Held at Howard University. New York: Lawrence Hill and Company, 1977.

Smith, Anthony. The Geopolitics of Information. New York: Oxford University Press, 1980.

Smith, Adam. The Wealth of Nations. Harmondsworth, England: Penguin Books, 1970.

Somavia, Juan, "International Communication and Third World Participation," Development Dialogue, no. 2 (1977), pp. 138-44.

Somavia, Juan. The Transnational Power Structure and International Information. Mexico City: ILET, 1978.

"South-South: A Necessary Alliance," South, no. 9 (July 1981), pp. 13-18.

"Statement by the Participants in the Dag Hammarskjöld Third World Journalist Seminar, New York, August 19-September 12, 1975," Development Dialogue, no. 1 (1976), p. 108.

Statistical Yearbook, 1980/1981. New York: United Nations, 1982.

Sterling, C.H., and Haight, T.R. The Mass Media: Aspen Institute Guide to Communication Industry Trends. New York: Praeger, 1978.

Stevenson, Robert L., "Beyond Belgrade: Prospects for a Balanced Flow of Information," a paper presented to the International Studies Association Annual Meeting, Philadelphia, PA, March 1981.

Stewart, Frances. Technology and Underdevelopment. London: Macmillan, 1977.

Stopford, John M.; Dunning, John H.; and Haberich, Klaus O. The World Directory of Multinational Enterprise. New York: Facts on File, 1980.

Stover, William James, and Anawalt, Howard C., "Who Makes News: An Inquiry into the Creation and Control of International Communication," Peace Research, vol. 15, no. 1 (January 1983), pp. 15-23, and no. 2 (June 1983), pp. 36-41.

Sulaiman, Ismail B., "Computers in Developing Countries: Malaysia's Experience," in Computers in Developing Nations, J.M. Bennett and R.E. Kalman, editors. Amsterdam: North Holland Publishing Company, 1981, pp. 237-42.

Sussman, Leonard R. Mass News Media and the Third World Challenge. London: Sage, 1977.

Systemes d'Informatique, May 1979.

"Technological Cooperation Between Developing Countries Including Exchange of Information and Experiences in Technology and Know-how Arrangements." Vienna, Austria: United Nations Industrial Development Organization, ID/W6, 271/1, 1978.

"Technological Self-Reliance of the Developing Countries: Toward Operational Strategies," Development and Transfer of Technology, series no. 15. Vienna, Austria: United Nations Industrial Development Organization, ID/262, 1981.

Tehranian, Majid. "Iran--Communication, Alienation, Revolution," Intermedia, vol. 7, no. 2 (March 1979), pp. 6-12.

Teilhard de Chardin, Pierre. The Future of Man. New York: Harper & Row, Publishers, 1964.

Telecommunications in Canada. Ottawa: National Parliament of Canada, Consultative Committee Report, April 1979.

Television and Behavior: Ten Years of Scientific Progress and Implications for the Eighties, vol. I. Washington, D.C.: National Institute of Mental Health, U.S. Department of Health and Human Services, 1982.

Thompson, Tina, "Get the Picture?," TRW Systems and Energy Magazine, vol. 5, no. 1 (Winter, 1981), pp. 12-17.

de Tocqueville, Alexis. Democracy in America, vol. II. New York: Alfred Knopf, 1948.

"Toward an American Agenda for a New World Order of Communications," A Conference Report of the United States National Commission for UNESCO. Washington, D.C.: Department of State, 1980.

"Towards a Strategy of Industrial Growth and Appropriate Technology." Vienna, Austria: United Nations Industrial Development Organization, ID/W6 264/1, 1978.

UNESCO Statistical Yearbook 1967. Paris: UNESCO, 1967.

UNESCO Statistical Yearbook 1974. Paris: UNESCO, 1974.

UNESCO Statistical Yearbook 1977. Paris: UNESCO, 1977.

UNESCO Statistical Yearbook 1981. Paris: UNESCO, 1981.

United Nations General Assembly, "False and Distorted Reports," Resolution 127 (II), November 5, 1947.

United Nations General Assembly, "The International Convention for the Protection of Civil and Political Rights," Resolution 2200A (XXI), December 16, 1966.

United Nations General Assembly, "Measures to be Taken Against Propaganda and the Inciters of a New War," Resolution 110 (II), November 3, 1947.

United Nations General Assembly. Universal Declaration of Human Rights, December 10, 1948.

United Nations General Assembly First Special Session on Disarmament, "Final Document" S-10/2, June 30, 1978.

United States Department of State. Report Submitted to Congress Pursuant to the Foreign Relations Authorization Act Fiscal Year 1979, Public law 95-426. Washington, D.C.: Government Printing Office, 1979.

Varis, Tapio, "World Information Order," Instant Research on Peace and Violence, vol. 4 (1976), pp. 143-47.

Weaver, David H.; Wilhoit, G. Cleveland; Stevenson, Robert L.; Shaw, Donald L.; and Cole, Richard R., "The News of the World in Four Major Wire Services," a paper for inclusion in the "Foreign Images" project of the International Association of Mass Communication Research for UNESCO, 1980.

Welch, Claude E., Jr., editor. Political Modernization. Belmont, Cal.: Wadsworth Publishing Co., 1971.

What Now? Another Development, Development Dialogue, no. 1 (1975), published by the Dag Hammarskjöld Foundation, Uppsala, Sweden.

Whiting, Gordon C., "How Does Communication Interface with Change?," in Communication and Development, Everett M. Rogers, editor. London: Sage, 1976, pp. 99-120.

Wiles, P. Distribution of Income--East and West. Amsterdam, The Netherlands: North Holland Publishing Company, 1974.

Yearbook of International Trade Statistics, 1980, vols. I and II. New York: United Nations, 1981.

Index